ARI

BEING

THE NARRATIVE OF

JOHN H. CADY
PIONEER

Rewritten and Revised by
BASIL DILLON WOON
1915

FOREWORD TO THE 1995 EDITION BY
L. BOYD FINCH

Republished by
Adobe Corral, Westerners International
Tucson, Arizona

Library of Congress
Cataloging-in-Publication Data
95-080406

Published by
Adobe Corral, Westerners International
Box 44220
Tucson, AZ 85733

Printed in the United States of America

TO

THE PIONEERS WHO ARE LIVING

AND TO

THE MEMORIES OF
THOSE WHO ARE DEAD

this book,

in affectionate tribute to the gallant courage, rugged independence and wonderful endurance of those adventurous souls who formed the vanguard of civilization in the early history of the Territory of Arizona and the remainder of the Great West,

is dedicated.

JOHN H. CADY
BASIL D. WOON

Patagonia,
     Arizona,
Nineteen-Fifteen.

FOREWORD

Pioneer in *une Toque Blanche*—
and a Writer in Two-Tone Shoes

THERE are at least two sure things concerning
John H. Cady: He was an Arizona pioneer,
and he was considered a culinary artist on
the frontier. Less than two years after his arrival
in Arizona he was selected to prepare a banquet for
Territorial Governor Richard C. McCormick.
Cady took pride in the title "chef"; he may even
have been Arizona's first gourmet chef.

His two-column advertisement in the December 27, 1912, issue of *The Santa Cruz Patagonian*
boasted:

> Best Services and Best Meals in Arizona
> ## THE PATAGONIA HOTEL
> Restaurant in Connection
> Rooms 50¢–75¢
> Meals a la Carte
> Chef Cady on the Range

Three years later, Cady paid a Los Angeles firm
to print his *Arizona's Yesterday*—a small gem that
describes life in early Arizona Territory. As far as
we know, the only reprint—which does not include
the preface—appeared in the Spring 1978 issue of
Old West magazine.[1]

Despite some questionable dates, Cady's memory was generally good. The names of nearly 100 pioneers appear in *Arizona's Yesterday* along with place names, some of which have since disappeared. While some of Cady's tales may not be literally, absolutely, true—many years had passed—much can be verified. In general, the flavor of frontier life is authentic.[2]

We cannot be as certain about who wrote the words that appear on the pages of Cady's book. The title page states: "Rewritten and Revised by BASIL DILLON WOON." This precocious English-born journalist also wrote the preface.

JOHN H. CADY

In October 1865, in Cincinnati, Ohio, nineteen-year-old Cady enlisted as a private in the Regular Army, Company C, First Cavalry. He was five feet, four and one-half inches tall. (Even in a time when men were shorter than they are today, only three other recruits listed on the forty-man register of enlistments were as short or shorter than Private Cady.) He signed his enlistment with an "X."[3]

Company C was shipped to the West Coast where it received mounts at Drum Barracks, San Pedro, California. The unit rode into Tucson in July 1866—nearly fourteen years before the railroad steamed into town, and well before January 1, 1870, the date that the Society of Arizona Pioneers later selected to define a "pioneer." Cady, however, was not a member of the society when it was formed in 1884; that may have been because of his absence from the territory (in California and Mexico) for a period after his army hitch was up in 1868. He did not apply for membership until 1906. Today's Arizona Historical Society, successor to the Pioneers' organization, holds only a very thin biographical file concerning him, plus several photos.

Most of what is known about Cady's life appears in the pages of *Arizona's Yesterday*. Fortunately, two recent books provide glimpses of the young Cady through the eyes of contemporaries: First Lt. Charles Henry Veil, his commanding officer; and George Hand, a fellow saloon keeper in Tucson.

Veil (Brevet Major "Vail" in Cady's book) became acting commander of Company C during the severe illness of Capt. William Dean (whom Cady mistakenly remembers as having remained in California when the company came to Arizona). In *The Memoirs of Charles Henry Veil: A Soldier's Recollections of the Civil War and the Arizona Territory*, edited by Herman J. Viola (New York: Orion Books, 1993), Veil praises Cady's culinary ability, declaring that he "was an extraordinarily good camp cook." How Cady came by his skills is not explained.

Veil also reveals that Cady was a mischief maker. Referring to an escapade that Cady leaves out of his book, the lieutenant describes an event in San

Pedro in June 1866, as Company C prepared to march to Tucson. "I remember the night after we received our horses," Veil wrote, "two men of my company (young boys) stole two of the best horses we had and made their escape." One of the AWOL soldiers was Cady.

The next day Veil started out in pursuit, trailing the pair for ninety miles in the direction of San Bernardino and then "across country toward foothills west of Chino Ranch." The lieutenant found Cady and his companion "lying asleep having worn out themselves and the horses." Veil concludes, "On account of their youth [they] were not court-martialed. Both served out their time. One afterward cooked for my mess and was an elegant cook."

According to Veil, Cady made excellent pies. Occasionally the officers' mess would indulge in the "expensive luxury" of a canned fruit pie, "but nearly every time we decided to do so, our pies would be stolen." For the Fourth of July, 1869 (probably Veil erred in the year since Cady's enlistment had expired the previous October), "the fruit was bought and the pies made, but when dinner came, Cady as usual reported the pies gone again, so we had no pie for dinner."

The next time Cady baked a pie, the post surgeon put a little croton oil, a drastic purgative, into the pie without Cady's knowledge. "Before dinner, the doctor was suddenly called for," Veil recalls. "Cady and his partner, the fellow with whom he had de-

serted from Drum Barracks, were reported very
sick. They were said to have had an attack of chol-
era or some similar disease, at least a very bad attack of diarrhea. The doctor called on Cady and
told him he would be all right 'as soon as he quit
eating so much pie. . . .' We had no trouble there-
after in the pie-stealing line." Although his pranks
got him in trouble with his commander, Cady in his
book praises Veil as the "highest type officer."[4]

Evidently, guests who sampled Chef Cady's civi-
lian cooking in later years concurred with Veil's
opinion of Cady's talents. In 1870, editor John
Wasson's *Arizona Citizen* reported: "The soiree at
Charley [*sic*] Foster's last evening was quite a suc-
cess; everyone present say they enjoyed it very
much. . . . Cady served up the supper and George
Hand did the agreeable behind the bar to match."[5]

Fortunately, for present-day Arizonans inter-
ested in Tucson's history, George Hand kept a remarkably candid diary, portions of which are in the
collections of the Arizona Historical Society. For
Hand's unvarnished account of life in "wild and
wooly" Tucson, readers owe thanks to editor Neil
Carmony for his painstaking and unexpurgated de-
ciphering of Hand's crabbed penmanship, published as *Whiskey, Six-Guns & Red-Light Ladies:*
George Hand's Saloon Diary, Tucson, 1875–1878
(Silver City, N.M.: High-Lonesome Books, 1994).

As a saloon keeper for many years, Hand must
have been one of his own best customers. If he

went to bed drunk, he recorded it so. If he bought the services of one of Tucson's prostitutes, he said so—and wrote down her first name and the price. And, perhaps most revealing of the times, if he or one of his friends had a night off, it was a noteworthy occasion: "went to bed sober." While Hand reported dozens of his friends drunk time and again, nowhere did he write that Cady was drunk.

Hand's reports of Cady are from 1875, a few years after Veil's experiences. Tucson was the territorial capital and Cady was, at various times, keeping a saloon and dance hall. In his January 12 entry Hand noted, "Sober today. . . . Cady and Jim Hart held a dance for the members of the legislature." Anyone who cares to speculate might wonder if, during the evening, Cady also provided female companions for the legislators.

On January 16 Hand reported, "John Cady reopened my old place on Main St.," a one-story adobe on a corner of Main and Congress streets. Two days later Hand wrote, "Went to a dance at Cady's, danced a few times, ate some lunch, and went home. . . . Carmel—$3.00."

On February 7 Hand noted, "Cady sold half his dance house," and on March 2 "Cady held a dance at the Halfway House." This was A. G. (A. C.?) Scott's roadhouse in the desert midway between Tucson and Camp (later Fort) Lowell. It, and Scott's racetrack, may have been in the vicinity of today's Alvernon Way and Speedway Boulevard.[6]

Although Hand and Cady do not seem to have been bosom buddies—many other Tucsonans appear more often in the diaries—on March 11 Hand recorded, "I ate supper with John Day at Cady's. Called on Mrs. Cady this afternoon." Nine days later Hand wrote, without providing details, "Cady broke my axe."

Mexican circuses and puppet shows (titeres) frequently played in Tucson. For April 13, 1875, Hand reported that "Professor LeRoy and the Mexican puppet show were hired by Cady to show in his corral." In this usage, Hand probably meant the patio or open space behind Cady's establishment.

It is not clear whether Cady had sold the saloon he opened in January or merely changed the operation, but on May 5 Hand reported, "Cady opened a bit house." According to editor Carmony, a bit house was "a saloon that sold a shot of rotgut whiskey for a 'bit' (12½¢), two shots for a quarter." Three days later Hand wrote: "Cady had music and a small monte game at his house. He made all the boys sick with his belly-wash." On another day: "Ate a pig's foot at Cady's and some Oregon apples." Cady also excelled at preparing pickled bull's feet, which he reported were a favorite at the Arizona City (Yuma) restaurant that he operated for a time. Yesterday's gourmet delicacies apparently met a different standard than today's.[7]

Cady states that he never "washed a [gold] pan" or owned a share in a mine. Instead, he preferred to open a business that miners would patronize. He must have been thinking along that line when Hand wrote for July 17, 1875: "Cady came back from the mines." Cady may have been visiting the booming town of Greaterville in the Santa Rita mountains south of Tucson, or the area that became known later as the Globe mining district. Hand noted on November 3, 1875, that "Cady sold his saloon to Simpson." Two days later Hand reported, "Cady and his lady left for the Gila settlements," possibly in the vicinity of Florence.[8]

Cady formed unions with several women. His first marriage, to a woman identified only as "Ruficia," ended in divorce. After this failure, Cady "determined to take no further chances with matrimony. However, I needed a helpmate, so I solved the difficulty by marrying Paola Ortega by contract for five years." He continues: "Contract marriages were universally recognized and indulged in in the West of the early days. . . . [At] the expiration of the contract . . . she went her way and I mine." This begs for more explanation. How common were contract marriages? Were they always for five years? Were they enforceable in court? Perhaps a student of Western women's history will find the answers.[9]

After John and Paola went their separate ways, Cady decided to take another chance at matrimony. In fact, he had two more wives. George Hand, who kept a list of deaths and violent events that covers more years than his surviving diaries, noted on December 21, 1886, "Georgia Cady died this evening of consumption." Hand probably meant Gregoria, whose death Cady remembered as occurring on December 23, 1889. Cady next married Paz Paredes, whom he called Donna Paz.[10]

As Arizona became more settled, Cady worked as a ranch hand and manager in what became Santa Cruz County (formed in 1899 from Pima County). In 1900 Cady, Paz, and their children, Mary (b. 1895) and Charles (b. 1899) moved to the new town of Patagonia, some five miles up Sonoita Creek. Patagonia, about eighteen miles northeast of Nogales, was then enjoying a mining boom.[11]

Cady built the first portion of his Patagonia Hotel, and resumed his role as host and chef. In the years that followed, he enlarged the hotel which he continued to operate until the 1920s when poor health caused him to move to California. After years of neglect, his hotel building was saved from demolition in 1947 when the Patagonia Woman's Club acquired the property and put it to use again as the town library, named Cady Hall. In the spring of 1995 it was renovated and expanded to better serve as a meeting hall as well as a library.[12]

On December 17, 1912, the *Santa Cruz Patagonian*, in describing a Christmas supper and dance at the Patagonia Hotel, shows that Cady's culinary abilities and reputation remained intact through the years. "A turkey supper was served, one of the kind Chef Cady knows how to prepare," the newspaper announced, "and it was thoroughly enjoyed."

By this time Cady wanted to look the part of an accomplished chef as well. Basil Woon tells how he met Cady at work at his hotel and wearing the "characteristic chef's top dress"—*une toque blanche*. After listening to some of the old pioneer's tales, Woon apparently recognized the opportunity for publication of "a straight, chronological and *intimate* description" of early life in Arizona. He proposed that Cady write an autobiography.

The first twenty or thirty pages of *Arizona's Yesterday*, recounting events before Cady's time in the territory, may be primarily Woon's work. Much of the rest of the book displays Woon's tendency to overwrite, imparting more romance and drama to Cady's frontier stories than crude reality would justify. In the eyes of Cady's fellow Arizonans, however, the published account that resulted was truly Cady's own. On December 18, 1915, the Nogales weekly newspaper, *The Border Vidette*, reported: "Captain John Cady, author of 'Arizona [*sic*] Yesterday,' now on the press, was here last Wednesday from Patagonia. The new book no doubt will sell like 'Hot Cakes.' It will be on sale sometime next month." An update on the following April 8 noted: "Captain John Cady is here from Patagonia distributing his book, 'Arizona of [*sic*] Yesterday'."

After publication of his book, Cady slipped quietly into old age. Paz died on October 22, 1919.

Following Mary's wedding to Thomas Kendall in 1924, Cady lived in the Los Angeles home of his daughter and son-in-law. He died April 8, 1927, in the Los Angeles Veterans' Hospital. [13]

BASIL DILLON WOON

It is noteworthy that Cady, whom Woon describes as a "grizzled old Indian fighter," welcomed the assistance of a man nearly half a century his junior. Born on September 28, 1893, in England, Basil Woon was only sixteen when he left home, seeking adventure in the wide world. He found it—first in Canada and then, a year later, in Alaska where he founded and edited the *Iditarod Weekly Prospector*, a gold-camp newspaper described by *The New York Times* as being *"north of Nome"* (emphasis added). Still in his teens, Woon soon afterward traveled to Reno, Nevada, where he covered the Jim Jeffries-Jack Johnson heavyweight fight. At that time the developing Mexican Revolution was the hottest news in the Western Hemisphere, attracting such writers as Ambrose Bierce and John Reed. Before many months had passed, the youthful Englishman also was roaming across Mexico, reporting the conflict for the United Press. [14]

Little is remembered about Woon in Arizona. His residence in the young state probably can be counted in months, not years. According to historian Alma Ready, Woon rode with Pancho Villa's

army as the representative of a New York newspaper, and then crossed the border to become city
editor of the *Nogales Daily Herald*.[15]

Issues of the *Herald* for this period are not avail-
able, but the *Border Vidette* provides bits of news
about Woon. The July 10, 1915, edition lists "Captain B. D. Woon" as one of the "illustrious adventurers" and prime movers of "The Adventurers'
Club," a new Nogales organization. In addition
to Woon, the founding members included Nogales
Mayor L. W. Mix and several men with military
titles—one "general," two "colonels," and a "major."
According to prevailing custom, the military titles
may have been honorific (note "Captain Cady").

The roving English journalist was only a year
older than Cady's daughter Mary, and long-time
Patagonia residents believe that the two shared a
mutual attraction. Mary's daughter, Frances M.
Kendall, confirms hearing firsthand that Woon
"courted my mother. She said she loved to dance
in her father's dance hall and had several suitors."[16]

Woon, however, was eager to move on. The
October 2, 1915, *Vidette* reported: "Today B. D.
Woon, printer, soldier of fortune and clever newspaper writer, will sever his connection with the
Nogales Daily Herald. From here Mr. Woon will
go to Cananea, thence to Tepic, Mexico, where he
will gather data for a story he has for a long time
been writing, on conditions in Mexico." Shortly
afterward, when *Arizona's Yesterday* came off the

press of the Los Angeles Times-Mirror Printing and Binding House, Woon was no longer in Arizona.

By age twenty, Woon had received a pilot's license, and during World War I he served overseas in the aviation section of the U.S. Signal Corps, forerunner of the Army Air Corps. The young aviator gained a charmed, romantic aura, having survived being shot down over Verdun, France, on his twenty-fifth birthday.

After the war, Woon joined the Universal News Service, becoming its chief Paris correspondent. In 1919 he married the first of his four wives. Along with other literary expatriates Woon lived in France for much of the 1920s. Unlike some of his contemporaries who presumably were better writers, he failed to make much literary history. [17]

In 1923–1924 Woon collaborated with Mme. Therese Berton, an off-and-on friend of "the Divine Sarah," to write *The Real Sarah Bernhardt Whom Her Audiences Never Knew*. The book is not totally adulatory, perhaps because Mme. Berton's husband Pierre was one of the actress's many bed partners. A reviewer in *The New York Times Book Review* commented that while "the reader may wish to take the biography at its face value . . . the utter absence of corroborating evidence from the thousand and one startling statements categorically made it a very definite obstacle." [18]

Woon followed *The Real Sarah Bernhardt* with European travel books touting prominent glamour spots and celebrity watering holes of the era. In the late 1920s he journeyed to Havana where he was director of the island government's tourist advertising and publicity. That sojourn resulted in the publication of *When It's Cocktail Time in Cuba*.[19]

Young Lawrence Clark Powell, a future literary light of the West and Tucson resident, meet Woon shortly after the Cuba episode. Powell remembers Woon among some thirty passengers on board the *Oregon*, a French freighter that sailed from San Pedro on Bastille Day (July 14, 1930) for a month-long voyage through the Panama Canal to Le Havre. Powell, who was working on his doctoral dissertation, closeted himself in his room for much of the voyage. He did not try to make friends with Woon, whom he now dismisses as "a hack travel writer."[20]

Returning to the States, Woon collaborated on another book, this time with Peggy Hopkins Joyce, a much-married, headline-grabbing showgirl whose tales enlivened *Men, Marriage and Me*. Attracted to Hollywood, the vagabond author wrote some forty-five screenplays, including (later) several for British filmmakers. Probably only the most devoted movie buffs remember Woon's work on *Recaptured Love, Men on Call, Two for Danger,* and *Rhythm Serenade*.[21]

Woon returned briefly to Arizona while researching a 1933 narrative guidebook: *Incredible Land: A Jaunty Baedeker to Hollywood and the Great*

Southwest. His tourist highlights included two paragraphs about Nogales and the scenery between there and Douglas. A cartoon-like illustration in the book depicts a dapper Woon standing near the Grand Canyon—high forehead, slicked-back dark hair, dark single-breasted jacket, light-colored trousers and two-tone shoes, evoking an early 1930s version of Fred Astaire.[22]

In 1936 Woon moved back to his native England where he was employed by the British Broadcasting Corporation. During World War II, he wrote such non-fiction titles as *Atlantic Front: The Merchant Navy in the War*; *Roosevelt, World Statesman*; and *Hell Came to London: A Reportage on the Blitz*. In the course of his long life, Woon wrote or co-uthored at least sixteen books, some of them for prominent publishers.[23]

Woon returned to the U.S. after the war, establishing his residence in Reno. There he wrote a Federated Features syndicated column: "The World and Basil Woon." The title demonstrates that the self-confident ego of Woon's teen years had not diminished. In addition, he broadcast his opinions on world affairs via a weekly radio program. In his last years, Woon produced a column for the *Nevada State Journal* and served as a publicity agent for several casinos.

Following a two-month illness, Woon died in a Reno hospital on June 4, 1974. He was eighty years old. His was not a dull life—chasing good stories

from Iditarod, Alaska, to Patagonia, Arizona, risk-
ing death by gunfire in the deserts of northern Mexico and in the skies over France, and scouting the
bistros of Paris and the casinos of Monte Carlo,
Havana, and Reno for the items that would make
the news wire or provide another chapter for a
book. Despite an eight-inch obituary in *The New
York Times*, Woon is scarcely remembered today.
An even longer obituary in *The Reno Evening
Gazette* provides still more details of a remarkable
life in which an aging Arizona pioneer supplied the
tales that enabled Woon to produce his first published book. This Adobe Corral reprint of *Arizona's Yesterday* is a fitting tribute to their unusual
collaboration and a rare glimpse into bygone days.[24]

L. BOYD FINCH

NOTES

The author is greatly indebted to Robert and Naomi Lenon
of Patagonia for information and suggestions that added
substantially to this account of the lives of John H. Cady,
his family, and Basil Dillon Woon.

1. John H. Cady, "Arizona's Yesterday," *Old West*, vol.
14 (Spring 1978): pp. 45–64.

2. As an example of unsubstantiated statements, on
pages 99–101 Cady gives the impression that he was an
active participant in the April 30, 1871 "Camp Grant Massacre," and on page 105 he claims that, at the time of writing
the book, he was "the only white survivor of that occurrence." However, he is not one of the named defendants in

the trial of the accused participants in the dawn attack in which "48 Mexicans, 6 Americans, and 94 Papagos" from the Tucson area killed eighty-five Pinal and Aravaipa Apaches (mostly women and children) who were peacefully camped near the military post. Possibly Cady was involved in some lesser way. The subsequent trial resulted in "not guilty" verdicts for all the defendants. Jay J. Wagoner, *Arizona Territory 1863–1912, a Political History* (Tucson: University of Arizona Press, 1970), pp. 129–131. Cady is not mentioned in the detailed account of the affair: Don Schellie, *Vast Domain of Blood: The Story of the Camp Grant Massacre* (Los Angeles: Westernlore Press, 1968).

3. Enlistment Declaration and Register of Enlistments, Records of the Adjutant General's Office, Record Group 94, National Archives.

4. Viola, ed., *Memoirs of Charles Henry Veil*, pp. 108–110. John H. Cady, *Arizona's Yesterday* (N.p.: Privately printed, 1916), p. 29.

5. Quoted in Schellie, *Vast Domain of Blood*, p. 61. Either Wasson or Schellie erred in identifying Hand's friend and occasional business partner, George Foster, as "Charley."

6. Carmony, ed., *Whiskey, Six-Guns & Red-Light Ladies*, pp. 30–41. A. C. [sic] Scott biographical file, Arizona Historical Society (AHS), Tucson. Although Hand's diary entries were published serially in bowdlerized form for many years in Tucson's *Arizona Daily Star*, Carmony's text is their first uncensored publication.

7. Carmony, pp. 42–47 passim.

8. Ibid, pp. 56, 68. Jim Simpson was proprietor of the Hole-in-the-Wall saloon at the corner of Meyer and Ochoa streets. It might have been another of Cady's locations.

9. Cady, *Arizona's Yesterday*, pp. 82–83. Two other

"contract marriages" occurred in the Southwest under different circumstances. Because of Arizona's anti-miscegenation law, former Lt. Henry O. Flipper, first black graduate of West Point, entered into a contract with Louisa Montoya in Nogales, Arizona, on Sept. 10, 1891; *Pima County Miscellaneous Records*, Book 4, pp. 536–537. Information about Flipper's marriage is elusive, but it appears that he and Louisa may have been "man and wife" for only a few months. To circumvent a military order requiring company laundresses to be married, Maria Baca entered into a contract marriage in the 1860s with a California Column private named Webber; three years later he was discharged and promptly left Maria and went off to Texas; Darlis A. Miller, *The California Column in New Mexico* (Albuquerque: University of New Mexico Press in cooperation with the Historical Society of New Mexico, 1982), p. 25.

10. Carmony, ed., *Whiskey, Six-Guns & Red-Light Ladies*, p. 243. Editor Carmony may have mistaken Hand's scribbled "Gregoria" for "Georgia."

11. Frances M. Kendall, Seal Beach, California, to L. Boyd Finch, February 27 and March 8, 1995, author's files. Paz Paredes Cady's two sons by a previous marriage, Daniel P. and John (Neves?), are believed to have adopted the Cady name. Paz is buried in Tucson's Holy Hope Cemetery. Cady continued operating his hotel for a time after her death. The author thanks Frances Kendall, the daughter of Mary Cady and Thomas Kendall and granddaughter of John and Paz, for graciously providing data for this family background. He also thanks Louise Easley of Patagonia for furnishing the address of Frances, her friend from childhood. Finch telephone conversation with Louise Easley, Patagonia, November 18, 1994.

12. The Cady Hall nomination for the National Register of Historic Places describes the building as a one-story plastered adobe. Originally the Patagonia Hotel, Cady Hall is identified as the oldest public-use building still standing in Patagonia.

13. John H. Cady biographical file, AHS. Frances M. Kendall to Finch, February 27 and March 8, 1995. Frances Kendall says that her grandfather and her parents shared a home about two miles from the Los Angeles Veterans' Hospital. An enclosed photograph shows that the only inscription on John Cady's gravestone in the Los Angeles Veterans' Cemetery, other than his name, is "U.S. Navy." This is surprising since Cady tells of going "over the hill" from his navy ship. Cady, *Arizona's Yesterday*, p. 48.

14. *The New York Times*, June 5, 1974; *The Reno Evening Gazette*, June 5, 1974.

15. Alma Ready, *Open Range and Hidden Silver: Arizona's Santa Cruz County* (Nogales: Alto Press, 1973), p. 79. One Arizonan remembers both Woon and Cady. Paul Holmes, now of Green Valley, born four years after Woon, recalls that the journalist chanced on Holmes and two other youths in Nogales, Arizona, and treated them to dinner at a hotel. Woon talked a lot about women in the ranchitas (houses of ill fame) of Nogales, Sonora, Holmes says. He adds that Woon enjoyed watching the dancers at Cady's Patagonia Hotel, and, in contrast to Woon's later apparent sophistication, in Nogales "he was not impressive looking, slovenly, never dressed up. We never took him very seriously . . . we thought he was a phony," Holmes concludes. The Green Valley resident recalls John Cady—"a typical old-timer" playing cards at a Patagonia pool hall. Finch telephone conversation with Paul Holmes, May 4, 1995.

16. Kendall to Finch, March 8, 1995.

17. *Reno Evening Gazette*, June 5, 1974.

18. Quoted in *The New York Times*, June 5, 1974.

19. *Reno Evening Gazette*, June 5, 1974.

20. Finch telephone conversation with Lawrence Clark Powell, Tucson, February 28, 1995.

21. Peggy Hopkins Joyce, *Men, Marriage and Me* (New York: The Macaulay Company, 1930); Jay Robert Nash and Stanley Ralph Ross, *The Motion Picture Guide* (Chicago: Cinebooks, Inc., 1987), p. I–3122.

22. Basil Woon, *Incredible Land: A Jaunty Baedeker to Hollywood and the Great Southwest* (New York: Liveright Corporation, 1933), p. 280.

23. *Reno Evening Gazette*, June 5, 1974. Woon's books in approximate order of publication are: *Arizona's Yesterday* (with Cady); *The Real Sarah Bernhardt* (with Therese Berton, editions published in both London and New York); *The Paris That's Not in the Guidebooks* (went into five printings); *The Frantic Atlantic*; *From Deauville to Monte Carlo, via LaTouquet, Biarritz, Vichy, Aix-les-Bains and Cannes*; *When It's Cocktail Time in Cuba*; *Men, Marriage and Me* (with Peggy Hopkins Joyce); *Incredible Land: A Jaunty Baedeker to Hollywood and the Great Southwest*; *San Francisco and the Golden Empire*; *Eyes West*; *Atlantic Front: The Merchant Navy in the War*; *Roosevelt, World Statesman*; *Hell Came to London: A Reportage of the Blitz*; *The Current Publishing Scene, Including Views of Trends for 1952*; *The Why, How, and Where of Gambling in Nevada*; *None of the Comforts of Home, But Oh, Those Cowboys*. Woon's major publishers included Knopf, Liveright, Brentano's and (in London) P. Davies.

24. *The New York Times*, June 5, 1974; *Reno Evening Gazette*, June 5, 1974.

*   *   *   *

Special thanks are due several members of The Adobe Corral of The Westerners who aided the research and writing of the Foreword: Olive Brand, Bruce Dinges, Jane Eppinga, Charles Herner, W. David Laird, Deloris Reynolds, and Virginia Culin Roberts Schlemme.

L. Boyd Finch is a native of Galesburg, Ill., with a B.A. from the University of Arizona and an M.A. in political science from Stanford University. His latest major publication, *Confederate Pathway to the Pacific: Major Sherod Hunter and Arizona Territory, C.S.A.*, is scheduled for publication in 1996 by the Arizona Historical Society, Tucson.

PREFACE

WHEN I first broached the matter of writing his autobiography to John H. Cady, two things had struck me particularly. One was that of all the literature about Arizona there was little that attempted to give a straight, chronological and *intimate* description of events that occurred during the early life of the Territory, and, second, that of all the men I knew, Cady was best fitted, by reason of his extraordinary experiences, remarkable memory for names and dates, and seniority in pioneership, to supply the work that I felt lacking.

Some years ago, when I first came West, I happened to be sitting on the observation platform of a train bound for the orange groves of Southern California. A lady with whom I had held some slight conversation on the journey turned to me after we had left Tucson and had started on the long and somewhat dreary journey across the desert that stretches from the "Old Pueblo" to "San Berdoo," and said:

"Do you know, I actually used to believe all those stories about the 'wildness of the West.' I see how badly I was mistaken."

She had taken a half-hour stroll about Tucson while the train changed crews and had been impressed by the—to the casual observer—sleepiness of the ancient town. She told me that never again would she look on a "wild West" moving picture without wanting to laugh. She would not believe that there had ever been a "wild West"—at least, not in Arizona. And yet it is history that the old Territory of Arizona in days gone by was the "wildest and woolliest" of all the West, as any old settler will testify.

There is no doubt that to the tourist the West is now a source of constant disappointment. The "movies" and certain literature have educated the Easterner to the belief that even now Indians go on the war-path occasionally, that even now cow-boys sometimes find an outlet for their exuberant spirits in the hair-raising sport of "shooting up the town," and that even now battles between the law-abiding cattlemen and the "rustlers" are more or less frequent. When these people come west in their comfortable Pullmans and discover nothing more interesting in the shape of Indians than a few old squaws selling trinkets and blankets on station platforms, as at Yuma; when they visit one of the famous old towns where in days gone by white men were wont to sleep with one eye and an ear open for marauding Indians, and find electric cars, modern office buildings, paved streets crowded with luxurious motors, and the inhabitants nonchalantly pursuing the even tenor of their ways garbed in habiliments strongly suggestive of Forty-fourth street and Broadway; when they come West and note these signs of an advancing and all-conquering civilization, I say, they invariably are disappointed. One lady I met even thought "how delightful" it would be "if the Apaches would only hold up the train!" It failed altogether to occur to her that, in the days when wagon-trains *were* held up by Apaches, few of those in them escaped to tell the gruesome tale. And yet this estimable lady, fresh from the drawing-rooms of Upper-Radcliffe-on-the-Hudson and the ballroom of Rector's, thought how "delightful" this would be! Ah, fortunate indeed is it that the pluck and persistence of the pioneers carved a way of peace for the pilgrims of today!

Considering the foregoing, such a book as this, presenting as it does in readable form the Arizona West as it *really was*, is, in my opinion, most opportune and fills a real need. The people have had fiction stories from the capable pens of Stewart Edward White and his companions in the realm of western literature, and have doubtless enjoyed their refreshing atmosphere and daring originality, but, despite this, fiction localized in the West and founded however-much on fact, does *not* supply all the needs of the Eastern reader, who demands the truth about those old days, presented in a compact and *intimate* form. I cannot too greatly emphasize that word "intimate," for it signifies to me the quality that has been most lacking in authoritative works on the Western country.

When I first met Captain Cady I found him the

very personification of what he ought not to have
been, considering the fact that he is one of the oldest
pioneers in Arizona.   Instead of peacefully awaiting
the close of a long and active career in some old
soldiers' home, I found him energetically superin-
tending the hotel he owns at Patagonia, Santa Cruz
county—and with a badly burned hand, at that.
There he was, with a characteristic chef's top-dress
on him (Cady is well known as a first-class cook),
standing behind the wood-fire range himself, per-
mitting no one else to do the cooking, allowing no
one else to shoulder the responsibilities that he, as a
man decidedly in the autumn of life, should by all
the rules of the "game" have long since relinquished.

Where this grizzled old Indian fighter, near his
three-score-and-ten, should have been white-haired,
he was but gray; where he should have been inflicted
with the kindred illnesses of advancing old age he
simply owned up, and sheepishly at that, to a burned
hand.   Where he should have been willing to lay
down his share of civic responsibility and let the
"young fellows" have a go at the game, he was as
ever on the firing-line, his name in the local paper a
half-dozen times each week.   Oh, no, it is wrong to
say that John H. Cady *was* a fighter—wrong in the
spirit of it, for, you see, he is very much of a fighter,
now.   He has lost not one whit of that aggressive-
ness and sterling courage that he always has owned,
the only difference being that, instead of fighting
Indians and bad men, he is now fighting the forces

of evil within his own town and contesting, as well,
the grim advances made by the relentless Reaper.

In travels that have taken me over a good slice
of Mother Earth, and that have brought me into
contact with all sorts and conditions of men, I have
never met one whose friendship I would rather have
than that of John H. Cady. If I were asked to sum
him up I would say that he is a *true* man—a true
father, a true and courageous fighter, and a true
American. He is a man anybody would far sooner
have with him than against him in a controversy.
If so far as world-standards go he has not achieved
fame—I had rather call it "notoriety"—it is because
of the fact that the present-day standards do not fit
the men whom they ignore. With those other men
who were the wet-nurses of the West in its infantile
civilization, this hardy pioneer should be honored
by the present generation and his name handed
down to posterity as that of one who fought the
good fight of progress, and fought well, with
weapons which if perhaps crude and clumsy—as the
age was crude and clumsy judged by Twentieth
Century standards—were at least most remarkably
effective.

The subject of this autobiography has traveled
to many out of the way places and accomplished
many remarkable things, but the most astonishing
thing about him is the casual and unaffected way in
which he, in retrospect, views his extraordinarily
active life. He talks to me as unconcernedly of

tramping hundreds of miles across a barren desert peopled with hostile Indians as though it were merely a street-car trip up the thoroughfares of one of Arizona's progressive cities. He talks of desperate rides through a wild and dangerous country, of little scraps, as he terms them, with bands of murderous Apaches, of meteoric rises from hired hand to ranch foreman, of adventurous expeditions into the realm of trade when everything was a risk in a land of uncertainty, of journeys through a foreign and wild country "dead broke"—of these and many similar things, as though they were commonplace incidents scarcely worthy of mention.

Yet the story of Cady's life is, I venture to state, one of the most gripping and interesting ever told, both from an historical and from a human point of view. It illustrates vividly the varied fortunes encountered by an adventurous pioneer of the old days in Arizona and contains, besides, historical facts not before recorded that cannot help making the work of unfailing interest to all who know, or wish to know, the State.

For you, then, reader, who love or wish to know the State of Arizona, with its painted deserts, its glorious skies, its wonderful mountains, its magical horizons, its illimitable distances, its romantic past and its magnificent possibilities, this little book has been written.

BASIL DILLON WOON.

CONTENTS

ILLUSTRATIONS

ARIZONA'S YESTERDAY

THE BOY SOLDIER

"For the right that needs assistance,
For the wrong that needs resistance,
For the future in the distance,
And the good that they could do."

FOURTEEN years before that broad, bloody line began to be drawn between the North and the South of the "United States of America," before there came the terrific clash of steel and muscle in front of which the entire world retreated to a distance, horrified, amazed, fascinated and confounded; before there came the dreadful day when families were estranged and birthrights surrendered, loves sacrificed and the blight of the bullet placed on hundreds of thousands of sturdy hearts— fourteen years before this, on the banks of the mighty Ohio at Cincinnati, I was born, on September 15, 1846. My parents were John N. Cady, of Cincinnati, and Maria Clingman Cady, who was of German descent, and of whom I remember little owing to the fact that she died when I reached my third birthday.

Ah, Cincinnati! To me you shall always be my City of Destiny, for it was within your boundaries that I, boy and man, met my several fates. One sent me through the turmoil and suffering of the Civil War; another sent me westward mounted on the wings of youthful hope and ambition. For that alone I am ever in the debt of Ohio's fairest city, which I hope to see again some day before there sounds for me the Taps. . . . But I do not know. The tide of life is more than past its ebb for me and I should be thinking more of a quiet rest on the hillside, my face turned to the turquoise blue of Arizona's matchless infinity, than to the treading again of noisy city streets in the country of my birth.

But this is to be a story of Arizona, and I must hasten through the events that occurred prior to my leaving for the West. When I had reached three years of age my father married again—a milliner— and moved to Philadelphia. My grandmother, who had raised me practically from birth, removed with me to Maysville in Kentucky, where I was sent to school. Some of my pleasantest memories now are of that period in the old-fashioned Kentucky river town.

Just after my ninth birthday my father came back to Maysville, claimed me, took me to Philadelphia with him and afterwards turned me over to one William Turner, his wife's brother, who was the owner of a farm on the eastern shore of Maryland. I stayed at the Turner farm until the outbreak of the Civil War in the fall of '61, when my father, who was then working for Devlin & Son, clothiers, with headquarters at Broadway and Warren streets, New York City, enlisted in Duryea's Zouaves as orderly sergeant in Company K. The Zouaves wintered at Federal Hill, Baltimore, and I joined my father and the regiment there. In the spring we moved to Washington, joining there the great Army of the Potomac, with which we stayed during that army's succession of magnificent battles, until after the Fredericksburg fight in '63.

In Washington we were quartered at Arlington Heights and I remember that I used to make pocket money by buying papers at the Washington railway depot and selling them on the Heights. The papers were, of course, full of nothing but war news, some of them owing their initial publication to the war, so great was the public's natural desire for news of the titanic struggle that was engulfing the continent. Then, as now, there were many conflicting statements as to the movements of troops, and so forth, but the war correspondents had full rein to write as they pleased, and the efforts of some of them stand out in my memory today as marvels of word-painting and penned rhetoric.

When Grant took command of the Army of the Potomac I left the army, three or four days before reinforcements for General Sherman, who was then making preparations for his famous "march to the sea," left for Kentucky. At Aguire Creek, near Washington, I purchased a cargo of apples for

$900—my first of two exceedingly profitable ventures in the apple-selling industry—and, after selling them at a handsome profit, followed Sherman's reinforcements as far as Cincinnati. I did not at this time stay long in the city of my birth, going in a few days to Camp Nelson, Ky., where I obtained work driving artillery horses to Atlanta and bringing back to Chattanooga condemned army stock. Even at that time—1864—the proud old city of Atlanta felt the shadow of its impending doom, but few believed Sherman would go to the lengths he did.

After the close of the war in 1865 I enlisted in Cincinnati, on October 12, in the California Rocky Mountain service. Before this, however, I had shipped in the Ram Vindicator of the Mississippi Squadron and after being transferred to the gunboat Syren had helped move the navy yard from Mound City, Ill., to Jefferson Barracks, St. Louis, Mo., where it still is.

I was drafted in the First United States Cavalry and sent to Carlisle Barracks in Pennsylvania, from which place I traveled to New Orleans, where I joined my regiment. I was allotted to Company C and remember my officers to have been Captain Dean, First Lieutenant Vail and Second Lieutenant Winters. Soon after my arrival in New Orleans we commenced our journey to California, then the golden country of every man's dreams and the Mecca of every man's ambition.

FOLLOWING THE ARGONAUTS

So it's Westward Ho! for the land of worth,
Where the "is," not "was" is vital;
Where brawn for praise must win the earth,
Nor risk its new-born title.
Where to damn a man is to say he ran,
And heedless seeds are sown,
Where the thrill of strife is the spice of life,
And the creed is "GUARD YOUR OWN!"

—WOON.

WHEN the fast mail steamer which had carried us from the Isthmus of Panama (we had journeyed to the Isthmus from New Orleans in the little transport McClellan), steamed through the Golden Gate and anchored off the Presidio I looked with great eagerness and curiosity on the wonderful city known in those days as "the toughest hole on earth," of which I had read and heard so much and which I had so longed to see. I saw a city rising on terraces from the smooth waters of a glorious bay whose wavelets were tempered by a sunshine that was as brilliant as it was ineffective against the keen sea-breeze of winter. The fog that had obscured our sight outside the Golden Gate was now gone—vanished like the mist-wraiths of the long-ago philosophers, and the glorious city of San Francisco was revealed to view.

I say "glorious," but the term must be understood
to apply only to the city's surroundings, which were
in truth magnificent. She looked like some imperial
goddess, her forehead encircled by the faint band of
mist that still lingered caressingly to the mountain
tops, her countenance glistening with the dew on
the green hill-slopes, her garments quaintly fash-
ioned for her by the civilization that had brought
her into being, her slippers the lustrous waters of
the Bay itself. Later I came to know that she, too,
was a goddess of moods, and dangerous moods;
a coquette to some, a love to others, and to many a
heartless vampire that sucked from them their hard-
wrung dust, scattered their gold to the four winds
of avarice that ever circled enticingly about the vor-
tex of shallow joys that the City harbored, and,
after intoxicating them with her beauty and her
wine, flung them aside to make ready for the next
comer. Too well had San Francisco merited the
title I give it in the opening lines of this chapter.
Some say that the earthquake and the fire came like
vitriol cast on the features of a beautiful woman for
the prostitution of her charms; but I, who lost little
to her lures, am not one to judge.

My memories of San Francisco are at any rate
a trifle hazy now, for it is many, many years since I
last saw the sun set over the Marin hills. An era
has passed since the glamour of the Coast of High
Barbaree claimed my youthful attention. But I
remember a city as evil within as it was lovely with-

out, a city where were gathered the very dregs of humanity from the four corners of the earth. What Port Said is now, San Francisco was then, only worse. For every crime that is committed in the dark alleys of the Suez port or the equally murky callejons of the pestholes of Mexico, four were committed in the beautiful Californian town when I first went there. Women as well as men carried "hardware" strapped outside, and scarcely one who had not at some time found this precaution useful. The city abounded with footpads and ruffians of every nationality and description, whose prices for cutting a throat or "rolling a stiff" depended on the cupidity of the moment or on the quantity of liquor their capacious stomachs held. Scores of killings occurred and excited little comment.

Thousands of men were daily passing in and out of the city, drawn by the lure of the Sierra goldfields; some of these came back with the joy of dreams come true and full pokes hung around their necks, some came with the misery of utter failure in their hearts, and some—alas, they were many, returned not at all.

The Barbary Coast was fast gaining for itself an unenviable reputation throughout the world. Every time one walked on Pacific street with any money in pocket he took his life in his hand. *"Guard Your Own!"* was the accepted creed of the time and woe to him who could not do so. Gold was thrown about like water. The dancing girls made fabulous

sums as commissions on drinks their consorts could
be persuaded to buy. Hundreds of thousands of dollars were spent nightly in the great temples devoted
to gambling, and there men risked on the luck of a
moment or the turn of a painted wheel fortunes
wrung from the soil by months and sometimes years
of terrific work in the diggings. The most famous
gamblers of the West at that time made their headquarters in San Francisco, and they came from all
countries. England contributed not a few of these
gentlemen traders in the caprices of fortune, France
her quota, Germany very few and China many; but
these last possessed the dives, the lowest kind of
gambling places, where men went only when they
were desperate and did not care.

We were not at this time, however, to be given an
opportunity to see as much of San Francisco as most
of us would have liked. After a short stay at the
Presidio we were sent to Wilmington, then a small
port in the southern part of the State but now incor-
porated in the great city of Los Angeles. Here we
drew our horses for the long trek across the desert
to our future home in the Territory of Arizona.
There was no railroad at that time in California, the
line not even having been surveyed as far as San
Jose, which was already a city but, instead of being,
as now, the market-place for a dozen fertile and
beautiful valleys, she was then merely an outfitting
point for parties of travelers, prospectors, cattlemen

OLD BARRACKS (1912) ON NORTH SIDE OF ALAMEDA STREET, NEAR MAIN, WHERE Co. C, 1st U. S. CAVALRY, CAMPED IN 1866 ON ITS ARRIVAL IN TUCSON

and the like, and was also a station and terminus for various stage lines.

Through San Jose, too, came those of the gold-seekers, bound for the high Sierras on the border of the desert, who had not taken the Sacramento River route and had decided to brave instead the dangers of the trail through the fertile San Joaquin, up to the Feather River and thus into the diggings about Virginia City. Gold had been found by that time in Nevada and hundreds of intrepid men were facing the awful Mojave and Nevada deserts, blazing hot in day-time and icy cold at night, to seek the new Eldorados. Since this is a book about pioneers, and since I am one of them, it is fitting to stay awhile and consider what civilization owes to these daring souls who formed the vanguard of her army. Cecil Rhodes opened an Empire by mobilizing a black race; Jim Hill opened another when he struck westward with steel rails. But the pioneers of the early gold rushes created an empire of immense riches with no other aid than their own gnarled hands and sturdy hearts. They opened up a country as vast as it was rich, and wrested from the very bosom of Mother Earth treasures that had been in her jealous keeping for ages before the era of Man. They braved sudden death, death from thirst and starvation, death from prowling savages, death from the wild creatures,—all that the works of man might flourish where they had not feared to tread.

It is the irony of fate that these old pioneers, many of whom hated civilization and were fleeing from her guiles, should have been the advance-guard of the very Power they sought to avoid.

The vast empire of Western America is strewn with the bones of these men. Some of them lie in kindly resting places, the grass over their graves kept green by loving friends; some lie uncared for in potters' fields or in the cemeteries of homes for the aged, and some—a vast horde—still lie bleached and grim, the hot sand drifted over them by the desert winds.

But, wherever they lie, all honor to the pioneer! There should be a day set apart on which every American should revere the memory of those men of long ago who hewed the way for the soft paths that fall to the generation of today.

What San Bernardino is now to the west-bound traveler, Wilmington was then—the end of the desert. From Wilmington eastward stretched one tremendous ocean of sand, interspersed here and there by majestic mountains in the fastnesses of which little fertile valleys with clear mountain streams were to be discovered later by the pioneer home-steaders. Where now are miles upon miles of yellow-fruited orange and lemon groves, betraying the care and knowledge of a later generation of scientific farmers, were then only dreary, barren wastes, with only the mountains and clumps of sagebrush, soapweed, cacti, creosote bushes and mesquite to break the everlasting monotony of the prospect.

Farming then, indeed, was almost as little thought of as irrigation, for men's minds were fixed on the star of whitest brilliancy—*Gold*. Men even made fortunes in the diggings and returned East and bought farms, never realizing that what might be pushed above the soil of California was destined to prove of far greater consequence than anything men would ever find hidden beneath.

The march to Arizona was both difficult and dangerous, and was to be attempted safely only by large parties. Water was scarce and wells few and far between, and there were several stretches as, for instance, that between what are now known as the Imperial Mountains and Yuma, of more than sixty miles with no water at all. The well at Dos Palmas was not dug until a later date. Across these stretches the traveler had to depend on what water he could manage to pack in a canteen strung around his waist or on his horse or mule. On the march were often to be seen, as they are still, those wonderful desert mirages of which so much has been written by explorers and scientists. Sometimes these took the form of lakes, fringed with palms, which tantalized and ever kept mockingly at a distance. Many the desert traveler who has been cruelly deceived by these mirages!

Yuma, of which I have just spoken, is famed for many reasons. For one thing, the story that United

States army officers "raised the temperature of the place thirty degrees" to be relieved from duty there, has been laughed at wherever Americans have been wont to congregate. And that old story told by Sherman, of the soldier who died at Yuma after living a particularly vicious existence here below, and who soon afterwards telegraphed from Hades for his blankets, has also done much to heighten the reputation of the little city, which sometimes still has applied to it the distinction of being the hottest place in the United States. This, however, is scarcely correct, as many places in the Southwest— Needles in California, and the Imperial Valley are examples—have often demonstrated higher temperatures than have ever been known at Yuma. A summer at the little Colorado River town is quite hot enough, however, to please the most tropical savage. It may be remarked here, in justice to the rest of the State, that the temperature of Yuma is not typical of Arizona as a whole. In the region I now live in—the Sonoita Valley in the southeastern part of the State, and in portions around Prescott, the summer temperatures are markedly cool and temperate.

Yuma, however, is not famed for its temperature alone; in fact, that feature of its claim to notice is least to be considered. The real noteworthy fact about Yuma from a historical point of view is that, as Arizona City, it was one of the earliest-settled points in the Territory and was at first easily the most important. The route of the major portion of the Forty-Niners took them across the Colorado River where Fort Yuma was situated on the California side; and the trend of exploration, business and commerce a few years later flowed westward to Yuma over the picturesque plains of the Gadsden Purchase. The famous California Column ferried itself across the Colorado at Yuma, and later on the Overland Mail came through the settlement. It is now a division point on the Southern Pacific Railway, just across the line from California, and has a population of three or four thousand.

At the time I first saw the place there was only Fort Yuma, on the California side of the river, and a small settlement on the Arizona side called Arizona City. It had formerly been called Colorado City, but the name was changed when the town was permanently settled. There were two ferries in operation at Yuma when our company arrived there, one of them run by the peaceable Yuma Indians and the other by a company headed by Don Diego Jaeger and Hartshorne. Fort Yuma had been established in 1851 by Major Heintzelman, U.S.A., but owing to scurvy (see De Long's history of Arizona) and the great difficulty in getting supplies, the Colorado River being then uncharted for traffic, it was abandoned and not permanently re-established until a year later, when Major Heintzelman returned from San Diego. The townsite of Colorado City was laid out in 1854, but floods wiped out the town with the result that a permanent settlement, called Arizona City, was not established until about 1862, four years before I reached there.

The first steamboat to reach Yuma with supplies was the Uncle Sam, which arrived in 1852. Of all this I can tell, of course, only by hearsay, but there is no doubt that the successful voyage of the Uncle Sam to Yuma established the importance of that place and gave it pre-eminence over any other shipping point into the territories for a long time.

Until the coming of the railroad, supplies for Arizona were shipped from San Francisco to the mouth of the Colorado and ferried from there up the river to Yuma, being there transferred to long wagon trains which traveled across the plains to Tucson, which was then the distributing point for the whole Territory.

Tucson was, of course, the chief city. I say "city" only in courtesy, for it was such in importance only, its size being smaller than an ordinary eastern village. Prescott, which was the first Territorial Capital; Tubac, considered by many the oldest settled town in Arizona, near which the famous mines worked by Sylvester Mowry were located; Ehrenberg, an important stage point; Sacaton, in the Pima and Maricopa Indian country, and other small settlements such as Apache Pass, which was a fort, were already in existence. The Gadsden Purchase having been of very recent date, most of the population was Indian, after which came the Mexicans and Spaniards and then the Americans, who arrogantly termed themselves the Whites, although the Spaniards possessed fully as white a complexion as the average pioneer from the eastern states. Until recently the Indian dominated the white man in Arizona in point of numbers, but fortunately only one Indian race—the Apache—showed unrelenting hostility to the white man and his works. Had all the Arizona Indians been as hostile as were the Apaches, the probabilities are that the settlement of Arizona by the whites would have been of far more recent date, for in instance after instance the Americans in Arizona were obliged to rely on the help of the peaceful Indians to combat the rapacious Apaches.

Yuma is the place where the infamous "Doc" Glanton and his gang operated. This was long before my time, and as the province of this book is merely to tell the story of life in the Territory as I saw it, it has no place within these pages. It may, however, be mentioned that Glanton was the leader of a notorious gang of freebooters who established a ferry across the Colorado at Yuma and used it as a hold-up scheme to trap unwary emigrants. The Yuma Indians also operated a ferry, for which they had hired as pilot a white man, whom some asserted to have been a deserter from the United States army. One day Glanton and his gang, angered at the successful rivalry of the Indians, fell on them and slew the pilot. The Glanton gang was subsequently wiped out by the Indians in retaliation.

When the Gila City gold rush set in Yuma was the point to which the adventurers came to reach the new city. I have heard that as many as three thousand gold seekers congregated at this find, but nothing is now to be seen of the former town but a few old deserted shacks and some Indian wickiups. Gold is still occasionally found in small quantities along the Gila River near this point, but the immense placer deposits have long since disappeared, although experts have been quoted as saying that the company brave enough to explore the fastnesses of the mountains back of the Gila at this point will probably be rewarded by finding rich gold mines.

I will not dwell on the hardships of that desert march from Yuma to Tucson, for which the rigors of the Civil War had fortunately prepared most of us, further than to say that it was many long, weary days before we finally came in sight of the "Old Pueblo." In Tucson I became, soon after our arrival, twenty years old. I was a fairly hardy youngster, too. We camped in Tucson on a piece of ground in the center of the town and soon after our arrival were set to work making a clean, orderly camp-park out of the wilderness of creosote bushes and mesquite. I remember that for some offence against the powers of the day I was then "serving time" for a short while and, among other things, I cut shrub on the site of Tucson's Military Plaza, with an inelegant piece of iron chain dangling uncomfortably from my left leg. Oh, I wasn't a saint

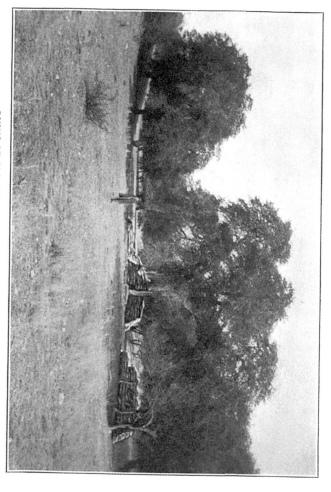

RUINS OF OLD FORT BUCHANAN, DECEMBER 7, 1914

in those days any more than I am a particularly
bright candidate for wings and a harp now! I gave
my superior officers fully as much trouble as the
rest of 'em!

Tucson's Military Plaza, it may be mentioned
here, was, as stated, cleared by Company C, First
United States Cavalry, and that body of troops was
the only lot of soldiery that ever camped on that
spot, which is now historic. In after years it was
known as Camp Lowell, and that name is still applied to a fort some seven miles east of Tucson.

Captain Dean had not come with us to Arizona,
having been taken ill in California and invalided
home. Lieutenant Vail, or, as he was entitled to be
called, Brevet-Major Vail, commanded Company C
in his absence, and he had under him as fearless a
set of men as could have been found anywhere in
the country in those days. Vail himself was the
highest type of officer—stern and unbending where
discipline was concerned, and eminently courageous.
Second Lieutenant Winters was a man of the same
stamp, and both men became well known in the Territory within a few months after their arrival because of their numerous and successful forays
against marauding Indians. Vail is alive yet, or
was a short time ago.

After some weeks in Tucson, which was then a
typical western town peopled by miners, assayers,
surveyors, tradespeople, a stray banker or two and,
last but not least by any means, gamblers, we were

moved to old Camp Grant, which was situated several hundred yards downstream from the point where the Aravaipa Creek runs into the San Pedro.

Among others whom I remember as living in Tucson or near neighborhood in 1866 were:

Henry Glassman,	Green Rusk,
Tom Yerkes,	Frank Hodge,
Lord & Williams,	Alex. Levin,
Pete Kitchen,	Bob Crandall,
— Tongue,	— Wheat,
The Kelsey boys,	Smith Turner,
Sandy McClatchy,	"Old" Pike.

Glassman lived most of the time at Tubac. Yerkes owned the Settlers Store in Tubac. Lord and Williams owned the chief store in Tucson and were agents for the United States Mail. Pete Kitchen was at Potrero Ranch; but Pete, who was more feared by the Indians than any white man in the Territory, deserves a whole chapter to himself. Tongue was a storekeeper. Green Rusk owned a popular dance house. Hodge and Levin had a saloon. Wheat owned a saloon and afterwards a ranch near Florence. The remainder were mostly gamblers, good fellows, every one of them. "Old Pike" especially was a character whose memory is now fondly cherished by every pioneer who knew him. He could win or lose with the same perpetual joviality, but he generally won. The principal gambling game in those days was Mexican monte, played with forty cards. Poker was also played a

great deal. Keno, faro and roulette were not intro-
duced until later, and the same may be said of
pangingi, the Scandinavian game.

There were several tribes of Apaches wintering
at Camp Grant the winter we went there, if I remember correctly, among them being the Tontos and
Aravaipas. All of them, however, were under the
authority of one chief—Old Eskiminzin, one of the
most blood-thirsty and vindictive of all the old
Apache leaders. The Government fed these Apaches
well during the winter in return for pledges they
made to keep the peace. This was due to the altru-
ism of some mistaken gentlemen in the councils of
authority in the East, who knew nothing of conditions in the Territory and who wrongly believed
that the word of an Apache Indian would hold good.
We, who knew the Indian, understood differently,
but we were obliged to obey orders, even though
these were responsible in part for the many Indian
tragedies that followed.

The Apache was a curious character. By nature
a nomad, by temperament a fighter, and from birth
a hater of the white man, he saw nothing good in
the ways of civilization except that which fed him,
and he took that only as a means to an end. Often
an Indian chief would solemnly swear to keep the
peace with his "white brethren" for a period of
months, and the next day go forth on a marauding
expedition and kill as many of his beloved "brethren" as he could lay his hands on. Every dead

white man was a feather in some Apache's head-
dress, for so they regarded it.

One day Chief Eskiminzin appeared with a protest from the tribes against the quality of the rations
they were receiving. It was early spring and the
protest, as we well knew, was merely his way of
saying that the Indians were no longer dependent on
what the government offered but could now hunt
their own meat. Our commanding officer endeavored to placate the old chief, who went back for a
conference with his men. Then he re-appeared,
threw down his rations, the others doing the same,
and in a few minutes the entire encampment of
Apaches was in the saddle.

Some little time after they had gone Lieutenant
Vail, suspecting trouble, sent a man down the trail
to investigate. A few miles away was a ranch
owned by a man named Israels. The scout found
the ranch devastated, with Israels, his wife and family brutally slain and all the stock driven off. He
reported to Vail, who headed an expedition of retaliation—the first I ever set forth on. We trailed the
Indians several days, finally coming up with them
and in a pitched battle killing many of them.

This was just a sample of the many similar incidents that occurred from time to time throughout
the Territory. Invariably the Military attempted to
find the raiders, and sometimes they were successful.
But it seemed impossible to teach the Apaches their
lesson, and even now there are sometimes simmer-

ings of discontent among the surviving Apaches on their reservation. They find it difficult to believe that their day and the day of the remainder of the savage Indian race is gone forever.

It was during this stay at Fort Grant that Company C was ordered to escort the first Southern Pacific survey from Apache Pass, which was a government fort, to Sacaton, in the Pima Indian country. The route abounded with hostile Apaches and was considered extremely dangerous. I have mentioned this as the "first Southern Pacific survey," but this does not mean that there were not before that other surveys of a similar character, looking to the establishment of a transcontinental railroad route through the Territory. As early as 1851 a survey was made across Northern Arizona by Captain L. Sitgreaves, approximating nearly the present route of the Santa Fe Railway. A year or two later Lieutenant A. W. Whipple made a survey along the line of the 35th degree parallel. Still later Lieutenant J. G. Parke surveyed a line nearly on that of the Southern Pacific survey. At that time, just before the Gadsden treaty, the territory surveyed was in the republic of Mexico. These surveys were all made by order of the then Secretary of War, Jefferson Davis, who aroused a storm of protest in the East against his "misguided attention to the desolate West." But few statesmen and fewer of the outside public in that day possessed the prophetic vision to perceive the future greatness of what were termed the "arid wastes" of Arizona and California. This was shown by the perfect hail of protest that swept to the White House when the terms of the Gadsden Treaty, drawn up by a man who as minister to a great minor republic had had ample opportunities to study at his leisure the nature of the country and the people with whom he dealt, became known.

This Southern Pacific survey party was under the superintendence of Chief Engineer Iego—I believe that is the way he spelled his name—who was recognized as one of the foremost men in his line in the country. The size of our party, which included thirty surveyors and surveyors' helpers in addition to the soldier escort, served to deter the Indians, and we had no trouble that I remember. It is perhaps worthy of note that the railroad, as it was afterwards built—it reached Tucson in 1880—did not exactly follow the line of this survey, not touching at Sacaton. It passed a few miles south of that point, near the famous Casa Grande, where now is a considerable town.

Railroad and all other surveying then was an exceedingly hazardous job, especially in Arizona, where so many Indian massacres had already occurred and were still to occur. In fact, any kind of a venture that involved traveling, even for a short distance, whether it was a small prospecting or emigrant's outfit or whether it was a long "train on hoofs," laden with goods of the utmost value, had to be escorted by a squad of soldiers, and often by an entire company. Even thus protected, frequent and daring raids were made by the cruel and fearless savages, whose only dread seemed to be starvation and the on-coming of the white man, and who would go to any lengths to get food.

Looking back in the light of present day reasoning, I am bound to say that it would be wrong to blame the Apaches for something their savage and untutored natures could not help. Before the "paleface" came to the Territory the Indian was lord of all he surveyed, from the peaks of the mountains down to the distant line of the silvery horizon. He was monarch of the desert and could roam over his demesne without interference save from hostile tribes; and into his very being there was born naturally a spirit of freedom which the white man with all his weapons could never kill. He knew the best hunting grounds, he knew where grew excellent fodder for his horses, he knew where water ran the year around, and in the rainy season he knew where the waterholes were to be found. In his wild life there was only the religion of living, and the divinity of Freedom.

When the white man came he, too, found the fertile places, the running water and the hunting grounds, and he confiscated them in the name of a higher civilization of which the savage knew nothing and desired to know less. Could the Indian then be blamed for his overwhelming hatred of the white man? His was the inferior, the barbaric race, to be sure, but could he be blamed for not believing so? His was a fight against civilization, true, and it was a losing fight as all such are bound to be, but the Indian did not know what civilization was except that it meant that he was to be robbed of his hunting grounds and stripped of his heritage of freedom. Therefore he fought tirelessly, savagely, demoniacally, the inroads of the white man into his territory. All that he knew, all that he wished to understand, was that he had been free and happy before the white man had come with his thunder-weapons, his fire-water and his mad, mad passion for yellow gold. The Indian could not understand or admit that the White was the superior, all-conquering race, and, not understanding, he became hostile and a battling demon.

———

So intense was the hatred of the white man among the Apaches of the period of which I speak that it was their custom to cut off the noses of any one of their women caught in illegal intercourse with a white man. This done, she was driven from her tribe, declared an outcast from her people, and frequently starved to death. I can remember many instances of this exact kind.

ROUGH AND TUMBLE ON LAND AND SEA

" 'Twas youth, my friend, and joyfulness besides,
That made me breast the treachery of Neptune's
*   fickle tides."*

WHEN Spring came around in the year 1867 we were moved to Tubac, where we were joined by K Company of my regiment and C Company of the Thirty-Second Infantry. Tubac, considered by some to be the oldest town in Arizona, before the consummation of the Gadsden Treaty was a military post at which the republic of Mexico regularly kept a small garrison. It was situated on the Santa Cruz River, which at this point generally had considerable water in it. This was probably the reason for the establishment of the town, for water has always been the controlling factor in a settlement's progress in Arizona. The river is dry at Tubac now, however, except in unusually rainy seasons, irrigation and cattle having robbed the stream of its former volume.

At the time we were quartered there Tubac was a place of no small importance, and after Tucson and Prescott were discounted it was probably the largest settlement in the Territory. Patagonia has now taken the position formerly occupied by the old adobe town as center of the rich mining zone of Southern Arizona, and the glories of Tubac (if they can be given that name) are, like the glories of Tombstone, gone. Unlike those of Tombstone, however, they are probably gone forever. Tombstone may yet rise from the ashes of her splendid past to a future as one of the important towns of the Southwest, if the stories of untold riches near by her are to be believed.

A little to the east of Tubac and separating that town from Patagonia is Mount Wrightson, one of the highest mountains in Arizona. Nicknamed "Old Baldy" after its famous namesake in California, this mammoth pile of rock and copper was in the old days a landmark for travelers, visible sometimes for days ahead on the wagon trails. It presaged near arrival in Tucson, for in a direct line Old Baldy is probably not further than forty miles from the Old Pueblo.

We camped at Tubac during the summer and part of the winter of 1867 and I remember that while we were there I cooked a reception banquet to Colonel Richard C. McCormick, who was then and until 1869 Governor of the Territory of Arizona. I forget his business in Tubac, but it was either an electioneering trip or one of inspection after his appointment to the office of Governor in 1866.

In the early part of 1868 we moved to Fort Buchanan, which before the war had been a military post of considerable importance. It received its name from the President before Lincoln and was garrisoned by Confederates during the Civil War. We re-built the fort and re-named it Fort Crittenden, in honor of General Thomas L. Crittenden, a son of the Hon. John J. Crittenden of Kentucky, who was then in command of the military district embracing that portion of the Territory south of the Gila River. Crittenden was beautifully situated on the Sonoita, about ten miles from where I now live and in the midst of some of the most marvelously beautiful scenery to be found on the American continent. Fort Crittenden is no longer occupied and has not been for some time; but a short distance toward Benson is Fort Huachuaca, where at present a garrison of the Ninth Cavalry is quartered.

During part of 1868 I carried mail from where Calabasas is now—it was then Fort Mason—to Fort Crittenden, a proceeding emphatically not as simple as it may sound. My way lay over a mountainous part of what is now Santa Cruz county, a district which at that time, on account of the excellent fodder and water, abounded with hostile Indians.

On one occasion that I well remember I had reached the waterhole over which is now the first railroad bridge north of Patagonia, about a half mile from the present town, and had stopped there to water my horse. While the animal was drinking I struck a match to light my pipe—and instantly I ducked. A bullet whistled over my head, near enough to give me a strong premonition that a couple of inches closer would have meant my end. I seized the bridle of my horse, leaped on his back, bent low over the saddle and rode for it. I escaped, but it is positive in my mind today that if those Apaches had been better accustomed to the use of the white man's weapons I would not now be alive to tell the story.

I was a great gambler, even in those days. It was the fashion, then, to gamble. Everybody except the priests and parsons gambled, and there was a scarcity of priests and parsons in the sixties. Men would gamble their dust, and when that was gone they would gamble their worldly possessions, and when those had vanished they would gamble their clothes, and if they lost their clothes there were instances where some men even went so far as to gamble their wives! And every one of us, each day, gambled his life, so you see the whole life in the Territory in the early days was one continuous gamble. Nobody save gamblers came out there, because nobody but gamblers would take the chance.

As I have stated, I followed the natural trend. I had a name, even in those days, of being one of the most spirited gamblers in the regiment, and that meant the countryside; and I confess it today without shame, although it is some time now since I raised an ante. I remember one occasion when my talents for games of chance turned out rather peculiarly. We had gone to Calabasas to get a load of wheat from a store owned by a man named Richardson, who had been a Colonel in the volunteer service. Richardson had as manager of the store a fellow named Long, who was well known for his passion for gambling. After we had given our order we sought about for some diversion to make the time pass, and Long caught sight of the goatskin chaperejos I was wearing. He stared at them enviously for a minute and then proposed to buy them.

"They're not for sale," said I, "but if you like I'll play you for 'em."

"Done!" said Long, and put up sixteen dollars against the chaps.

Now, Long was a game sport, but that didn't make him lucky. I won his sixteen dollars and then he bet me some whiskey against the lot, and again I won. By the time I had beat him five or six times, had won a good half of the store's contents, and was proposing to play him for his share in the store itself, he cried quits. We loaded our plunder on the wagon. Near Bloxton, or where Bloxton now is, four miles west of Patagonia, we managed to upset the wagon, and half the whiskey and wheat never was retrieved. We had the wherewithal to "fix things" with the officers, however, and went unreproved, even making a tidy profit selling what stuff we had left to the soldiers.

At that time the company maintained gardens on a part of what afterwards was the Sanford Rancho, and at one time during 1868 I was gardening there with three others. The gardens were on a ranch owned by William Morgan, a discharged sergeant of our company. Morgan had one Mexican working for him and there were four of us from the Fort stationed there to cultivate the gardens and keep him company—more for the latter reason than the first, I believe. We took turn and turn about of one month at the Fort and one month at the gardens, which were about fourteen miles from the Fort.

One of us was Private White, of Company K. He was a mighty fine young fellow, and we all liked him. Early one morning the five of us were eating breakfast in the cabin, an illustration of which is given, and White went outside for something. Soon afterward we heard several reports, but, figuring that White had shot at some animal or other, we did not even get up from our meal. Finally came another shot, and then another, and Morgan got up and peered from the door. He gave a cry.

"Apaches!" he shouted. "They're all around! Poor White——"

It was nip-and-tuck then. For hours we kept up a steady fire at the Indians, who circled the house with blood-curdling whoops. We killed a number of them before they finally took themselves off. Then we went forth to look for White. We found our comrade lying on his back a short distance away, his eyes staring unseeingly to the sky. He was dead. We carried him to the house and discussed the situation.

"They'll come back," said Morgan, with conviction.

"Then it's up to one of us to ride to the Fort," I said.

But Morgan shook his head.

"There isn't a horse anywhere near," he said.

We had an old army mule working on the gardens and I bethought myself of him.

"There's the mule," I suggested.

My companions were silent. That mule was the slowest creature in Arizona, I firmly believed. It was as much as he could do to walk, let alone gallop.

"Somebody's got to go, or we'll all be killed," I said. "Let's draw lots."

They agreed and we found five straws, one of them shorter than the rest. These we drew, and the short one fell to me.

I look back on that desperate ride now with feelings akin to horror. Surrounded with murderous savages, with only a decrepit mule to ride and fourteen miles to go, it seemed impossible that I could get through safely. My companions said good-bye to me as though I were a scaffold victim about to be executed. But get through I did—how I do not know—and the chillingly weird war-calls of the Indians howling at me from the hills as I rode return to my ears even now with extraordinary vividness.

And, as Morgan had prophesied, the Apaches did "come back." It was a month later, and I had been transferred back to the Fort, when a nephew of Colonel Dunkelberger and William J. Osborn of

Tucson were riding near Morgan's ranch. Apaches ambushed them, slew the Colonel's nephew, whose name has slipped my memory, and wounded Osborn. The latter, who was a person of considerable importance in the Territory, escaped to Morgan's ranch. An expedition of retaliation was immediately organized at the Fort and the soldiers pursued the assassins into Mexico, finally coming up with them and killing a number. I did not accompany the troops on this occasion, having been detailed to the Santa Rita range to bring in lumber to be used in building houses.

I returned from the Santa Ritas in July and found an order had been received at the Fort from the War Department that all men whose times had expired or were shortly to expire should be congregated in Tucson and from there marched to California for their discharge. A few weeks later I went to the Old Pueblo and, together with several hundred others from all parts of the Territory, was mustered out and started on the return march to Wilmington where we arrived about October 1. On the twelfth of October I was discharged.

After working as cook for a short time for a company that was constructing a railroad from Wilmington to Los Angeles, I moved to the latter place and obtained employment in the Old Bella Union Hotel as chef. John King was the proprietor of the Bella Union. Until Christmas eve I stayed there, and then Sergeant John Curtis, of my company, who

CADY'S HOUSE ON THE SONOITA, NEAR BLOXTON, 1914. BUILT IN 1868

had been working as a saddler for Banning, a cap-
italist in Wilmington, came back to the kitchen and
said:

"John, old sport, let's go to 'Frisco."

"I haven't," I told him, "enough change to set 'em
up across the street, let alone go to 'Frisco."

For answer Curtis pulled out a wallet, drew therefrom a roll of bills that amounted to about $1,000,
divided the pile into two halves, laid them on the
table and indicated them with his forefinger.

"John," he offered, "if you'll come with me you
can put one of those piles in your pocket. What do
you say?"

Inasmuch as I had had previously little opportunity to really explore San Francisco, the idea ap-
pealed to me and we shook hands on the bargain.
Christmas morning, fine, cloudless and warm, found
us seated on the San Jose stage. San Jose then was
nearly as large a place as Tucson is now—about
twenty odd thousand, if I remember rightly. The
stage route carried us through the mission country now so widely exploited by the railroads.
Santa Barbara, San Luis Obispo and Monterey were
all towns on the way, Monterey being probably the
largest. The country was very thinly occupied,
chiefly by Spanish haciendas that had been in the
country long before gold was discovered. The few
and powerful owners of these estates controlled
practically the entire beautiful State of California
prior to '49, and at the time I write of still retained

a goodly portion of it. They grew rich and powerful, for their lands were either taken by right of con-
quest or by grants from the original Mexican government, and they paid no wages to their peons.
These Spaniards, with the priests, however, are to
be credited with whatever progress civilization made
in the early days of California. They built the first
passable roads, they completed rough surveys and
they first discovered the wonderful fertility of the
California soils. The towns they built were built
solidly, with an eye to the future ravages of earth-
quakes and of Time, which is something the modern
builder often does not do. There are in many of
their pueblos old houses built by the Spaniards in
the middle part of the eighteenth century which are
still used and occupied.

We arrived in San Francisco a few days after our
departure from Los Angeles, and before long the
city had done to us what she still does to so many—
had broken us on her fickle wheel of fortune. It
wasn't many days before we found ourselves, our
"good time" a thing of the past, "up against it."

"John," said Curtis, finally, "we're broke. We
can't get no work. What'll we do?"

I thought a minute and then suggested the only
alternative I could think of. "Let's get a blanket,"
I offered.

"Getting a blanket" was the phrase commonly in
use when men meant to say that they intended to
enlist. Curtis met the idea with instant approval, if

not with acclamation, and, suiting the action to the words, we obtained a hack and drove to the Presidio, where we underwent the examination for artillerymen. Curtis passed easily and was accepted, but I, owing to a wound in my ankle received during the war, was refused.

Curtis obtained the customary three days' leave before joining his company and for that brief space we roamed about the city, finishing our "good time" with such money as Curtis had been able to raise by pawning and selling his belongings. After the three days were over we parted, Curtis to join his regiment; and since then I have neither seen nor heard of him. If he still chances to be living, my best wishes go out to him in his old age.

For some time I hung around San Francisco trying to obtain employment, without any luck. I was not then as skillful a gambler as I became in after years, and, in any case, I had no money with which to gamble. It was, I found, one thing to sit down to a monte deck at a table surrounded with people you knew, where your credit was good, and another to stake your money on a painted wheel in a great hall where nobody cared whether you won or lost.

Trying to make my little stake last as long as possible, I roomed in a cheap hotel—the old What Cheer rooming house, and ate but one "two-bit" meal a day. I was constantly on the lookout for work of some kind, but had no luck until one day as I was passing up Kearney street I saw a sign in one of the store windows calling for volunteers for the Sloop-o'-War Jamestown. After reading the notice a couple of times I decided to enlist, did so, was sent to Mare Island Navy Yard and from there boarded the Jamestown.

It was on that vessel that I performed an action that I have not since regretted, however reprehensible it may seem in the light of present-day ethics. Smallpox broke out on board and I, fearful of contracting the dread disease, planned to desert. This would probably not have been possible today, when the quarantine regulations are so strict, but in those days port authorities were seldom on the alert to prevent vessels with diseases anchoring with other shipping, especially in Mexico, in the waters of which country we were cruising.

When we reached Mazatlan I went ashore in the ordinary course of my duties as ward-room steward to do some marketing and take the officers' laundry to be washed. Instead of bringing the marketing back to the ship I sent it, together with a note telling where the laundry would be found, and saying goodbye forever to my shipmates. The note written and dispatched, I quietly "vamoosed," or, as I believe it is popularly termed in the navy now, I "went over the hill."

My primary excuse for this action was, of course, the outbreak of smallpox, which at that time and in fact until very recently, was as greatly dreaded as bubonic plague is now, and probably more. Vaccination, whatever may be its value in the prevention of the disease, had not been discovered in the sense that it is now understood and was not known at all except in the centers of medical practice in the East.

Smallpox then was a mysterious disease, and certainly a plague. Whole populations had been wiped out by it, doctors had announced that there was practically no cure for it and that its contraction meant almost certain death, and I may thus be excused for my fear of the sickness. I venture to state, moreover, that if all the men aboard the Jamestown had had the same opportunity that I was given to desert, they would have done so in a body.

My second excuse, reader, if one is necessary, is that in the days of the Jamestown and her sister ships, navy life was very different from the navy life of today, when I understand generous paymasters are even giving the jackies ice-cream with their meals. You may be entirely sure that we got nothing of the kind. Our food was bad, our quarters were worse, and the discipline was unbearably severe.

THROUGH MEXICO AND BACK TO ARIZONA

"Know thou the spell of the desert land,
Where Life and Love are free?
Know thou the lure the sky and sand
Hath for the man in me?"

WHEN I deserted from the sloop-o'-war Jamestown it was with the no uncertain knowledge that it was distinctly to my best advantage to clear out of the city of Mazatlan just as rapidly as I could, for the ships of the free and (presumably) enlightened Republic had not yet swerved altogether from the customs of the King's Navee, one of which said customs was to hang deserters at the yard-arm. Sometimes they shot them, but I do not remember that the gentlemen most concerned had any choice in the matter. At any rate, I know that it was with a distinct feeling of relief that I covered the last few yards that brought me out of the city of Mazatlan and into the open country. In theory, of course, the captain of the sloop-o'-war Jamestown could not have sent a squad of men after me with instructions to bring me back off foreign soil dead or alive, but in practice that is just what he would have done. Theory and practice have a habit of differing, especially in the actions of an irate skipper who sees one of his best ward-room stewards vanishing from his jurisdiction.

Life now opened before me with such a vista of possibilities that I felt my breath taken away. Here was I, a youth twenty-two years old, husky and sound physically, free in a foreign country which I felt an instant liking for, and no longer beholden to the Stars and Stripes for which I was quite ready to fight but not to serve in durance vile on a plague-ship. My spirit bounded at the thought of the liberty that was mine, and I struck northward out of Mazatlan with a light step and a lighter heart. At the edge of the city I paused awhile on a bluff to gaze for the last time on the Bay, on the waters of which rode quietly at anchor the vessel I had a few hours before quit so unceremoniously. There was no regret in my heart as I stood there and looked. I had no particular love for Mexico, but then I had no particular love for the sea, either, and a good deal less for the ships that sailed the sea. So I turned my back very definitely on that part of my life and set my face toward the north, where, had I known it, I was to find my destiny beneath the cloudless turquoise skies of Arizona.

When I left Mazatlan it was with the intention of walking as far as I could before stopping, or until the weight of the small bundle containing my worldly possessions tired my shoulders. But it was not to be so. Only two miles out of the city I came upon a ranch owned by two Americans, the sight of whom was very welcome to me just then. I had no idea that I should find any American ranchers in the

near neighborhood, and considered myself in luck.
I found that one of the American's names was Colonel Elliot and I asked him for work.   Elliot sized
me up, invited me in to rest up, and on talking with
him I found him to be an exceedingly congenial soul.
He was an old Confederate colonel—was Elliot, but
although we had served on opposite sides of the sad
war of a few years back, the common bond of nationality that is always strongest beyond the con-
fines of one's own land prevented us from feeling
any aloofness toward each other on this account.
To me Colonel Elliot was an American, and a mighty
decent specimen of an American at that—a friend
in need.   And to Colonel Elliot also I was an American, and one needing assistance.   We seldom spoke
of our political differences, partly because our lives
speedily became too full and intimate to admit of
the petty exchange of divergent views, and partly
because I had been a boy during the Civil War and
my youthful brain had not been sufficiently mature
to assimilate the manifold prejudices, likes, dislikes
and opposing theories that were the heritage of
nearly all those who lived during that bloody four
years' war.

I have said that Colonel Elliot was a friend in
need.   There is an apt saying that a "friend in need
is a friend indeed," and such was Colonel Elliot as
I soon found.   For I had not been a week at the
ranch when I was struck down with smallpox, and
throughout that dangerous sickness, lasting several

weeks, the old Colonel, careless of contagion, nursed me like a woman, finally bringing me back to a point where I once again had full possession of all my youthful health and vigor.

I do not just now recall the length of time I worked for Elliot and his partner, but the stay, if not long, was most decidedly pleasant. I grew to speak Spanish fluently, haunted the town of Mazatlan (from which the Jamestown had long since departed), and made as good use generally of my temporary employment as was possible. I tried hard to master the patois of the peon as well as the flowery and eloquent language of the aristocracy, for I knew well that should I at any time seek employment as overseer at a rancho either in Mexico or Arizona, a knowledge of the former would be indispensable, while a knowledge of the latter was at all times useful in Mexico, especially in the cities, where the possession of the cultured dialect marked one for special favors and secured better attention at the stores.

The Mexicans I grew to understand and like more and more the longer I knew them. I found the average Mexican gentleman a model of politeness, a Beau Brummel in dress and an artist in the use of the flowery terms with which his splendid language abounds. The peons also I came to know and understand. I found them a simple-minded, uncomplaining class, willingly accepting the burdens which were laid on them by their masters, the rich landlords; and living, loving and playing very much as

children.   They   were   good-hearted—these   Mexicans, and hospitable to the last degree. This, indeed,
is a characteristic as truly of the Mexican of today
as of the period of which I speak. They would, if
needs be, share their last crust with you even if you
were an utter   stranger, and many the time some
lowly peon host of mine would insist on my occupy-
ing his rude bed whilst he and his family slept on
the roof! Such warm-hearted simplicity is very
agreeable, and it was a vast change from the world
of the Americans, especially of the West, where the
watchword was: "Every man for himsel', and the
de'il tak' the hindmost."   It may be remarked here
that the de'il often took the foremost, too!

When I left the hospitable shelter of Colonel Elliot's home I moved to Rosario, Sinaloa, where was
situated the famous Tajo mine which has made the
fortunes of the Bradbury family.   It was owned
then by Don Luis Bradbury, senior, the same Bradbury whose son is now such a prominent figure in
the social and commercial life of San Francisco and
Los Angeles.   I asked for work at the Bradbury
mine, obtained it, and started in shoveling refuse
like any other common laborer at the munificent
wage of ten dollars per week, which was a little less
than ten dollars more than the Mexican peons labor-
ing at the same work obtained.   I had not been
working there long, however, when some suggestions I made to the engineer obtained me recognition
and promotion, and at the end of a year, when I

quit, I was earning $150 per month, or nearly four times what my wage had been when I started.

And then—and then, I believe it was the spell of the Arizona plains that gripped the strings of my soul again and caused them to play a different tune. . . . Or was it the prospect of an exciting and more or less lawless life on the frontier that beckoned with enticing lure? I do not know. But I grew to think more and more of Arizona, the Territory in which I had reached my majority and had found my manhood; and more and more I discovered myself longing to be back shaking hands with my old friends and companions, and shaking, too, dice with Life itself. So one day saw me once more on my way to the wild and free Territory, although this time my road did not lie wholly across a burning and uninhabited desert.

It is a hard enough proposition now to get to the United States from Mazatlan, or any other point in Mexico, when the Sud Pacifico and other railroads are shattered in a dozen places and their schedules, those that have them, are dependent on the magnanimity of the various tribes of bandits that infest the routes; but at the time I write of it was harder.

To strike north overland was possible, though not to be advised, for brigands infested the cedar forests of Sinaloa and southern Sonora; and savage Yaquis, quite as much to be feared as the Apaches of further north, ravaged the desert and mountain country. I solved the difficulty finally by going to Mazatlan

and shipping from that port as a deck-hand on a
Dutch brigantine, which I remember because of its
exceptionally vile quarters and the particularly dirty
weather we ran up against on our passage up the
Gulf. The Gulf of California, especially the mouth
of it, has always had an evil reputation among
mariners, and with justness, but I firmly believe the
elements out-did themselves in ferocity on the trip
I refer to.

Guaymas reached, my troubles were not over, for
there was still the long Sonora desert to be crossed
before the haven of Hermosillo could be reached.
At last I made arrangements with a freighting outfit
and went along with them. I had had a little money
when I started, but both Mazatlan and Guaymas
happened to be chiefly filled with cantinas and
gambling-hells, and as I was not averse to frequent-
ing either of these places of first resort to the lonely
wanderer, my money-bag was considerably depleted
when at last I arrived in the beautiful capital of
Sonora. I was, in fact, if a few odd dollars are
excepted, broke, and work was a prime necessity.
Fortunately, jobs were at that time not very hard
to find.

There was at that time in Hermosillo a house
named the Casa Marian Para, kept by one who
styled himself William Taft. The Casa Marian
Para will probably be remembered in Hermosillo by
old-timers now—in fact, I have my doubts that it is
not still standing. It was the chief stopping-house

in Sonora at that time. I obtained employment from Taft as a cook, but stayed with it only long enough to procure myself a "grub-stake," after which I "hit the grit" for Tucson, crossing the border on the Nogales trail a few days later. I arrived in Tucson in the latter part of the year 1870, and obtained work cooking for Charlie Brown and his family.

It was while I was employed as chef in the Brown household that I made—and lost, of course, a fortune. No, it wasn't a very big fortune, but it was a fortune certainly very curiously and originally made. I made it by selling ham sandwiches!

Charlie Brown owned a saloon not far from the Old Church Plaza. It was called Congress Hall, had been completed in 1868 and was one of the most popular places in town. Charlie was fast becoming a plutocrat. One night in the saloon I happened to hear a man come in and complain because there wasn't a restaurant in town that would serve him a light snack at that time of night except at outrageous prices.

"That's right," said another man near me, "if somebody would only have the sense to start a lunch-counter here the way they have them in the East he'd make all kinds of money."

The words suggested a scheme to me. The next day I saw Brown and got his permission to serve a light lunch of sandwiches and coffee in the saloon after I had finished my work at the house. Just at that time there was a big crowd in the town, the first cattle having arrived in charge of a hungry lot of Texan cowpunchers, and everyone was making money. I set up my little lunch counter, charged seventy-five cents, or "six-bits" in the language of the West, for a lunch consisting of a cup of coffee and a sandwich, and speedily had all the customers I could handle. For forty consecutive nights I made a clear profit of over fifty dollars each night. Those sandwiches were a mint. And they were worth what I charged for them, too, for bacon, ham, coffee and the other things were 'way up, the three mentioned being fifty or sixty cents a pound for a very indifferent quality.

Sometimes I had a long line waiting to buy lunches, and all the time I ran that lunch stand I never had one "kick" at the prices or the grub offered. Those cowboys were well supplied with money, and they were more than willing to spend it. Charlie Brown was making his fortune fast.

After I quit Brown's employ, John McGee—the same man who now is secretary of the Arizona Pioneers' Historical Society and a well-known resident of Tucson—hired myself and another man to do assessment work on the old Salero mine, which had been operated before the war. Our conveyance was an old ambulance owned by Lord & Williams, who, as I have said, kept the only store and the postoffice in Tucson. The outfit was driven by "Old Bill" Sniffen, who will doubtless be remembered by many Arizona pioneers. We picked up on the way "Old

Man" Benedict, another familiar character, who kept the stage station and ranch at Sahuarita, where the Twin Buttes Railroad now has a station and branch to some mines, and where a smelter is located. We were paid ten dollars per day for our work and returned safely to Tucson.

I spoke of Lord & Williams' store just now. When in the city of Tucson recently I saw that Mr. Corbett has his tin shop where the old store and post-office was once. I recognized only two other buildings as having existed in pioneer days, although there may be more. One was the old church of San Augustine and the other was part of the Orndorff Hotel, where Levin had his saloon. There were more saloons than anything else in Tucson in the old days, and the pueblo richly earned its reputation, spread broadcast all over the world, as being one of the "toughest" places on the American frontier.

Tucson was on the boom just then. Besides the first shipment of cattle, and the influx of cowboys from Texas previously mentioned, the Territorial capital had just been moved to Tucson from Prescott. It was afterwards moved back again to Prescott, and subsequently to the new town of Phoenix; but more of that later.

After successfully concluding the assessment work and returning to Tucson to be paid off by McGee I decided to move again, and this time chose Wickenburg, a little place between Phoenix and Prescott,

and one of the pioneer towns of the Territory.
West of Wickenburg on the Colorado River was
another settlement named Ehrenberg, after a man
who deserves a paragraph to himself.

Herman Ehrenberg was a civil engineer and sci-
entist of exceptional talents who engaged in mining
in the early days of Arizona following the occupation of the Territory by the Americans. He was of
German birth and, coming at an early age to the
United States, made his way to New Orleans, where
he enlisted in the New Orleans Grays when war
broke out between Mexico and Texas. After serving in the battles of Goliad and Fanning's Defeat he
returned to Germany and wrote and lectured for
some time on Texas and its resources. Soon after
the publication of his book on Texas he returned to
the United States and at St. Louis, in 1840, he
joined a party crossing to Oregon. From that Territory he went to the Sandwich Islands and for some
years wandered among the islands of the Polyne-
sian Archipelago, returning to California in time to
join General Fremont in the latter's attempt to free
California from Mexican rule. After the Gadsden
Purchase he moved to Arizona, where, after years
of occupation in mining and other industries, he was
killed by a Digger Indian at Dos Palmas in Southern California. The town of Ehrenberg was named
after him.*

*This information relative to Ehrenberg is taken largely
from The History of Arizona; De Long, 1905.

FORT CRITTENDEN RUINS, 1914. QUARTERS OF Cos. K AND C, 1st U. S. CAVALRY IN 1868

STAGE DRIVER'S LUCK

God, men call Destiny: Hear thee my prayer!
Grant that life's secret for e'er shall be kept.
Wiser than mine is thy will; I dare
Not dust where thy broom hath swept.
—WOON.

I HAVE said that Wickenburg was a small place half-way between Phoenix and Prescott, but that is not quite right. Wickenburg was situated between Prescott and the valley of the Salt River, in the fertile midst of which the foundation stones of the future capital of Arizona had yet to be laid. To be sure, there were a few shacks on the site, and a few ranchers in the valley, but the city of Phoenix had yet to blossom forth from the wilderness. I shall find occasion later to speak of the birth of Phoenix, however.

When I arrived in Wickenburg from Tucson— and the journey was no mean affair, involving, as it did, a ride over desert and mountains, both of which were crowded with hostile Apaches—I went to work as stage driver for the company that operated stages out of Wickenburg to Ehrenberg, Prescott and other places, including Florence which was just then beginning to be a town.

Stage driving in Arizona in the pioneer days was a dangerous, difficult, and consequently high-priced

job. The Indians were responsible for this in the
main, although white highwaymen became somewhat numerous later on. Sometimes there would be
a raid, the driver would be killed, and the stage
would not depart again for some days, the company
being unable to find a man to take the reins. The
stages were large and unwieldy, but strongly built.
They had to be big enough to hold off raiders should
they attack. Every stage usually carried, besides
the driver, two company men who went heavily
armed and belted around with numerous cartridges.
One sat beside the driver on the box-seat. In the
case of the longer stage trips two or three men
guarded the mail. Very few women traveled in
those days—in fact, there were not many white
women in the Territory and those who did travel
usually carried some masculine protector with them.
A man had to be a good driver to drive a stage, too,
for the heavy brakes were not easily manipulated
and there were some very bad stretches of road.

Apropos of what I have just said about stage
drivers being slain, and the difficulty sometimes ex-
perienced in getting men to take their places, I remember that on certain occasions I would take the
place of the mail driver from Tucson to Apache
Pass, north of where Douglas now is—the said mail
driver having been killed—get fifty dollars for the
trip and blow it all in before I started for fear I
might not otherwise get a chance to spend it.

The stage I drove for this Wickenburg company

was one that ran regular trips out of Wickenburg. Several trips passed without much occurring worthy of note; and then on one trip I fell off the box, injuring my ankle. When I arrived back in Wickenburg I was told by Manager Pierson of the company that I would be relieved from driving the stage because my foot was not strong enough to work the heavy brakes, and would be given instead the buckboard to drive to Florence and back on postoffice business.

The next trip the stage made out of Wickenburg, therefore, I remained behind. A few miles from town the stage was held up by an overwhelming force of Apaches, the driver and all save two of the passengers massacred, and the contents looted. A woman named Moll Shepherd, going back East with a large sum of money in her possession, and a man named Kruger, escaped the Indians, hid in the hills and were the only two who survived to tell the story of what has gone down into history as the famous "Wickenburg Stage Massacre." I shudder now to think how nearly I might have been on the box on that fatal trip.

I was not entirely to escape the Apaches, however. On the first return trip from Florence to Wickenburg with the buckboard, while I was congratulating myself and thanking my lucky stars for the accident to my ankle, Apaches "jumped" the buckboard and gave me and my one passenger, Charlie Block of Wickenburg, a severe tussle for it. We beat them off in the end, owing to superior marksmanship, and arrived in Wickenburg unhurt. Block was part owner of the Barnett and Block store in Wickenburg and was a well-known man in that section.

After this incident I determined to quit driving stages and buckboards and, casting about for some new line of endeavor, went for the first time into the restaurant business for myself. The town needed an establishment of the kind I put up, and as I had always been a good cook I cleaned up handsomely, especially as it was while I was running the restaurant that Miner started his notorious stampede, when thousands of gold-mad men followed a will-o'-the-wisp trail to fabulously rich diggings which turned out to be entirely mythical.

It was astonishing how little was required in those days to start a stampede. A stranger might come in town with a "poke" of gold dust. He would naturally be asked where he had made the strike. As a matter of fact, he probably had washed a dozen different streams to get the poke-full, but under the influence of liquor he might reply: "Oh, over on the San Carlos," or the San Pedro, or some other stream. It did not require that he should state how rich the streak was, or whether it had panned out. All that was necessary to start a mad rush in the direction he had designated was the sight of his gold and the magic word "streak." Many were the trails that led to death or bitter disappointment, in Arizona's early days.

Most of the old prospectors did not see the results

of their own "strikes" nor share in the profits from them after their first "poke" had been obtained. There was old John Waring, for instance, who found gold on a tributary of the Colorado and blew into Arizona City, got drunk and told of his find:

"Gold—Gold. . . . Lots 'v it!" he informed them, drunkenly, incoherently, and woke up the next morning to find that half the town had disappeared in the direction of his claim. He rushed to the registry office to register his claim, which he had foolishly forgotten to do the night before. He found it already registered. Some unscrupulous rascal had filched his secret, even to the exact location of his claim, from the aged miner and had got ahead of him in registering it. No claim is really legal until it is registered, although in the mining camps of the old days it was a formality often dispensed with, since claim jumpers met a prompt and drastic punishment.

In many other instances the big mining men gobbled up the smaller ones, especially at a later period, when most of the big mines were grouped under a few large managements, with consequent great advantage over their smaller competitors.

Indeed, there is comparatively little incentive now for a prospector to set out in Arizona, because if he chances to stumble on a really rich prospect, and attempts to work it himself, he is likely to be so browbeaten that he is finally forced to sell out to some large concern. There are only a few smelters in or near the State and these are controlled by large mining companies. Very well; we will suppose a hypothetical case:

A, being a prospector, finds a copper mine. He says to himself: "Here's a good property; it ought to make me rich. I won't sell it, I'll hold on to it and work it myself."

So far, so good.

A starts in to work his mine. He digs therefrom considerable rich ore. And now a problem presents itself.

He has no concentrator, no smelter of his own. He cannot afford to build one; therefore it is perfectly obvious that he cannot crush his own ore. He must, then, send it elsewhere to be smelted, and to do this must sell his ore to the smelter.

In the meantime a certain big mining company has investigated A's find and has seen that it is rich. The company desires the property, as it desires all other rich properties. It offers to buy the mine for a sum far below its actual value. Naturally, the finder refuses.

But he must smelt his ore. And to smelt it he finds he is compelled to sell it to a smelter that is controlled by the mining company whose offer he has refused. He sends his ore to the smelter. Back comes the quotation for his product, at a price ridiculously low. "That's what we'll give you," says the company, through its proxy the smelter, "take it or leave it," or words to that effect.

Now, what can A do? Nothing at all. He must either sell his ore at an actual loss or sell his mine to the company. Naturally, he does the latter, and at a figure he finds considerably lower than the first offer. The large concern has him where it wanted him and it snuffs out his dreams of wealth and prosperity effectively.

These observations are disinterested. I have never, curiously enough, heeded the insistent call of the diggings; I have never "washed a pan," and my name has never appeared on the share-list of a mine. And this, too, has been in spite of the fact that often I have been directly in the paths of the various excitements. I have been always wise enough to see that the men who made rapid fortunes in gold were not the men who stampeded head-over-heels to the diggings, but the men who stayed behind and opened up some kind of business which the gold-seekers would patronize. These were the reapers of the harvest, and there was little risk in their game, although the stakes were high.

I have said that I never owned a mining share. Well, I never did; but once I came close to owning a part share in what is now the richest copper mine on earth—a mine that, with the Anaconda in Montana, almost determines the price of raw copper. I will tell you the tale.

Along in the middle seventies—I think it was '74, I was partner with a man named George Stevens at Eureka Springs, west of Fort Thomas in the

Apache country, a trading station for freighters.
We were owners of the trading station, which was
some distance south of where the copper cities of
Globe and Miami are now situated. We made very
good money at the station and Stevens and I decided
to have some repairs and additions built to the store.
We looked around for a mason and finally hired
one named George Warren, a competent man whose
only fault was a fondness for the cup that cheers.

Warren was also a prospector of some note and
had made several rich strikes. It was known that,
while he had never found a bonanza, wherever he
announced "pay dirt" there "pay dirt" invariably
was to be found. In other words, he had a reputation for reliability that was valuable to him and of
which he was intensely vain. He was a man with
"hunches," and hunches curiously enough, that
almost always made good.

These hunches were more or less frequent with
Warren. They usually came when he was broke
for, like all prospectors, Warren found it highly
inconvenient ever to be the possessor of a large sum
of money for any length of time. He had been
known to say to a friend: "I've got a hunch!" dis-
appear, and in a week or two, return with a liberal
amount of dust. Between hunches he worked at his
trade.

When he had completed his work on the store at
Eureka Springs for myself and Stevens, Warren
drew me aside one night and, very confidentially, in-

formed me that he had a hunch. "You're welcome to it, George," I said, and, something calling
me away at that moment, I did not hear of him
again until I returned from New Fort Grant,
whither I had gone with a load of hay for which we
had a valuable contract with the government. Then
Stevens informed me that Warren had told him of
his hunch, had asked for a grub-stake, and, on being
given one, had departed in a southerly direction with
the information that he expected to make a find over
in the Dos Cabezas direction.

He was gone several weeks, and then one day
Stevens said to me, quietly:

"John, Warren's back."

"Yes?" I answered. "Did he make a strike?"

"He found a copper mine," said Stevens.

"Oh, only copper!" I laughed. "That hunch sys-
tem of his must have got tarnished by this time,
then!"

You see, copper at that time was worth next to
nothing. There was no big smelter in the Territory
and it was almost impossible to sell the ore. So it
was natural enough that neither myself nor Stevens
should feel particularly jubilant over Warren's
strike. One day I thought to ask Warren whether
he had christened his mine yet, as was the custom.

"I'm going to call it the 'Copper Queen,'" he said.

I laughed at him for the name, but admitted it a
good one. That mine today, reader, is one of the
greatest copper properties in the world. It is worth

about a billion dollars.   The syndicate that owns it owns as well a good slice of Arizona.

"Syndicate?" I hear you ask.   "Why, what about Warren, the man who found the mine, and Stevens, the man who grub-staked him?"

Ah! What about them! George Stevens bet his share of the mine against $75 at a horse race one day, and lost; and George Warren, the man with the infallible hunch, died years back in squalid misery, driven there by drink and the memory of many empty discoveries.   The syndicate that obtained the mine from Warren gave him a pension amply sufficient for his needs, I believe.   It is but fair to state that had the mine been retained by Warren the probabilities are it would never have been developed, for Warren, like other old prospectors, was a genius at finding pay-streaks, but a failure when it came to exploiting them.

That, reader, is the true story of the discovery of the Copper Queen, the mine that has made a dozen fortunes and two cities—Bisbee and Douglas. If I had gone in with Stevens in grub-staking poor Warren would I, too, I wonder, have sold my share for some foolish trifle or recklesssly gambled it away? I wonder! .   .   .   .   .   .   Probably, I should.

A FRONTIER BUSINESS MAN

"The chip of chisel, hum of saw,
  The stones of progress laid;
The city grew, and, helped by its law,
  Men many fortunes made."
          —Song of the City, by T. BURGESS.

A PHOENIX man was in Patagonia recently and—I don't say he was a typical Phoenix man—commented in a superior tone on the size of the town.

"Why," he said, as if it clinched the argument, "Phoenix would make ten Patagonias."

"And then some," I assented, "but, sonny, I built the third house in Phoenix. Did you know that? And I burnt Indian grain fields in the Salt River Valley long before anyone ever thought of building a city there. Even a big city has had some time to be a small one."

That settled it; the Phoenix gentleman said no more.

I told him only the exact truth when I said that I built the third house in Phoenix.

After I had started the Wickenburg restaurant came rumors that a new city was to be started in the fertile Salt River Valley, between Sacaton and Prescott, some forty or fifty miles north of the former place. Stories came that men had tilled the land of the valley and had found that it would grow almost anything, as, indeed, it has since been found that any land in Arizona will do, providing the water is obtained to irrigate it. One of Arizona's most wonderful phenomena is the sudden greening of the sandy stretches after a heavy rain. One day everything is a sun-dried brown, as far as the eye can see. Every arroyo is dry, the very cactus seems shriveled and the deep blue of the sky gives no promise of any relief. Then, in the night, thunder-clouds roll up from the painted hills, a tropical deluge resembling a cloud-burst falls, and in the morning—lo! where was yellow sand parched from months of drought, is now sprouting green grass! It is a marvelous transformation—a miracle never to be forgotten by one who has seen it.

However, irrigation is absolutely necessary to till the soil in most districts of Arizona, though in some sections of the State dry farming has been successfully resorted to. It has been said that Arizona has more rivers and less water than any state in the Union, and this is true. Many of these are rivers only in the rainy season, which in the desert generally comes about the middle of July and lasts until early fall. Others are what is known as "sinking rivers," flowing above ground for parts of their courses, and as frequently sinking below the sand, to reappear further along. The Sonoita, upon which Patagonia is situated, is one of these "disappearing rivers," the water coming up out of the sand about half a mile from the main street.   The big rivers, the Colorado, the Salt, the upper Gila and the San Pedro, run the year around, and there are several smaller streams in the more fertile districts that do the same thing.

The larger part of the Arizona "desert" is not barren sand, but fertile silt and adobe, needing only water to make of it the best possible soil for farming purposes.   Favored by a mild winter climate the Salt River Valley can be made to produce crops of some kind each month in the year—fruits in the fall, vegetables in the winter season, grains in spring and alfalfa, the principal crop, throughout the summer. A succession of crops may oftentimes be grown during the year on one farm, so that irrigated lands in Arizona yield several times the produce obtainable in the Eastern states.   Alfalfa may be cut six or seven times a year with a yield of as much as ten tons to the acre.   The finest Egyptian cotton, free from the boll weevil scourge, may also be grown successfully and is fast becoming one of the staple products of the State.   Potatoes, strawberries, pears, peaches and melons, from temperate climates; and citrus fruits, sorghum grains and date palms from subtropical regions, give some idea of the range of crops possible here. Many farmers from the Eastern and Southern states and from California, finding this out, began to take up land, dig irrigating ditches and make homes in Arizona.

Fifteen or twenty pioneers had gone to the Salt

River Valley while I was at Wickenburg and there had taken up quarter sections on which they raised, chiefly, barley, wheat, corn and hay. A little fruit was also experimented in. Some of the men who were on the ground at the beginning I remember to have been Dennis and Murphy, Tom Gray, Jack Walters, Johnny George, George Monroe, Joe Fugit, Jack Swilling, Patterson, the Parkers, the Sorrels, the Fenters and a few others whose names I do not recall. A townsite had been laid out, streets surveyed, and before long it became known that the Territory had a new city, the name of which was Phoenix.

The story of the way in which the name "Phoenix" was given to the city that in future days was to become the metropolis of the State, is interesting. When the Miner excitement was over I decided to move to the new Salt River townsite, and soon after my arrival there attended a meeting of citizens gathered together to name the new city. Practically every settler in the Valley was at this meeting, which was destined to become historic.

Among those present was a Frenchman named Darrel Dupper, or Du Perre, as his name has sometimes been written, who was a highly educated man and had lived in Arizona for a number of years. When the question of naming the townsite came up several suggestions were offered, among them being "Salt City," "Aricropolis," and others. Dupper rose to his feet and suggested that the city be called

Phoenix, because, he explained, the Phoenix was a bird of beautiful plumage and exceptional voice, which lived for five hundred years and then, after chanting its death-song, prepared a charnel-house for itself and was cremated, after which a new and glorified bird arose from the ashes to live a magnificent existence forever. When Dupper finished his suggestion and explanation the meeting voted on the names and the Frenchman's choice was decided upon. "Phoenix" it has been ever since.

Before I had been in Phoenix many days I commenced the building of a restaurant, which I named the Capital Restaurant. The capital was then at Prescott, having been moved from Tucson, but my name evidently must have been prophetic, for the capital city of Arizona is now none other than Phoenix, which at the present day probably has the largest population in the State—over twenty thousand.

Soon I gained other interests in Phoenix besides the restaurant. The Capital made me much money, and I invested what I did not spend in "having a good time," in various other enterprises. I went into the butcher business with Steel & Coplin. I built the first bakery in Phoenix. I staked two men to a ranch north of the city, from which I later on proceeded to flood the Territory with sweet potatoes. I was the first man, by the way, to grow sweet potatoes in Arizona. I built a saloon and dance hall, and in this, naturally, was my quickest turnover.

I am not an apologist, least of all for myself, and

as this is the true story of a life I believe to have been exceptionally varied I think that in it should be related the things I did which might be considered "bad" nowadays, as well as the things I did which, by the same token, present-day civilization may consider "good."

I may relate, therefore, that for some years I was known as the largest liquor dealer in the Territory, as well as one of the shrewdest hands at cards. Although I employed men to do the work, often players would insist on my dealing the monte deck or laying down the faro lay-out for them. I played for big stakes, too—bigger stakes than people play for nowadays in the West. Many times I have sat down with the equivalent of thousands of dollars in chips and played them all away, only to regain them again without thinking it anything particularly unusual. As games go, I was considered "lucky" for a gambler. Though not superstitious, I believed in this luck of mine, and this is probably the reason that it held good for so long. If of late various things, chiefly the mining depression, have made my fortunes all to the bad, I am no man to whine at the inevitable. I can take my ipecac along with the next man!

There were few men in the old days in Phoenix, or, indeed, the entire Territory, who did not drink liquor, and lots of it. In fact, it may be said that the entire fabric of the Territory was constructed on liquor. The pioneers were most of them whiskey

THE OLD WARD HOMESTEAD, WHERE CADY KEPT STORE
DURING THE BUILDING OF THE SANTA FE RAILROAD

fiends, as were the gamblers. By this I am not defending the liquor traffic. I have sold more liquor than any man in Arizona over the bar in my lifetime, but I voted dry at the last election and I adhere to the belief that a whiskey-less Arizona will be the best for our children and our children's children.

During my residence in Phoenix Darrel Dupper, the man who had christened the town, became one of my best friends. He kept the post and trading store at Desert Station, at which place was the only water to be found between Phoenix and Wickenburg, if I remember correctly. The station made him wealthy. Dupper was originally Count Du Perre, and came of a noted aristocratic French family. His forefathers were, I believe, prominent in the court of Louis XIV. When a young man he committed some foolhardy act in France and was banished by his people, who sent him a monthly remittance on condition that he get as far away from his home as he could, and stay there. To fulfill the terms of this agreement Du Perre came to Arizona among the early pioneers and soon proved that he had the stuff of a real man in him. He learned English and Americanized his name to Dupper. He engaged in various enterprises and finally started Desert Station, where he made his fortune.

He was a curious character as he became older. Sometimes he would stay away from Phoenix for several months and then one day he would appear with a few thousand dollars, more or less, spend every cent of it in treating the boys in my house and "blow back" home again generally in my debt. He used to sing La Marseillaise—it was the only song he knew—and after the first few drinks would solemnly mount a table, sing a few verses of the magnificent revolutionary song, call on me to do likewise, and then "treat the house." Often he did this several times each night, and as "treating the house" invariably cost at least thirty dollars and he was an inveterate gambler, it will be seen that in one way or another I managed to secure considerable of old Dupper's fortune. His partiality to the Marseillaise leads me to the belief that he was banished for participation in one of the French revolutions; but this I cannot state positively.

On one occasion I remember that I was visiting with Dupper and we made a trip together somewhere, Dupper leaving his cook in charge. When we returned nobody noticed us and I happened to look through a window before entering the house. Hastily I beckoned to Dupper.

The Frenchman's cook was sitting on his bed with a pile of money—the day's takings—in front of him. He was dividing the pile into two halves. Taking one bill off the pile he would lay it to one side and say:

"This is for Dupper."

Then he'd take the next bill, lay it in another spot, and say:

"And this is for me."

We watched him through the window unnoticed until he came to the last ten-dollar bill. It was odd. The cook deliberated a few moments and finally put the bill on top of the pile he had reserved for himself. Then Dupper, whose face had been a study in emotions, could keep still no longer.

"Hey, there!" he yelled, "play fair—play fair! Divvy up that ten spot!"

What happened afterwards to that cook I don't remember. But Dupper was a good sport.

VENTURES AND ADVENTURES

Hush! What brooding stillness is hanging over all?
What's this talk in whispers, and that placard on
*   the wall?*
Aha! I see it now! They're going to hang a man!
Judge Lynch is on the ramparts and the Law's an
*   "Also-Ran!"*   —WOON.

R EADER, have you ever seen the look in a
    man's eyes after he has been condemned by
    that Court of Last Appeal—his fellow-men?
I have, many times. It is a look without a shadow
of hope left, a look of dread at the ferocity of the
mob, a look of fear at what is to come afterwards;
and seldom a hint of defiance lurks in such a man's
expression.

I have seen and figured in many lynchings. In
the old days they were the inseparables, the Frontier
and Judge Lynch. If a white man killed a Mexican
or Indian nothing was done, except perhaps to hold
a farce of a trial with the killer in the end turned
loose; and if a white man killed another white man
there was seldom much outcry, unless the case was
cold-blooded murder or the killer was already unpop-
ular. But let a Mexican or an Indian lift one finger
against a white man and the whole strength of the
Whites was against him in a moment; he was
hounded to his hole, dragged forth, tried by a com-

mittee of citizens over whom Judge Lynch sat with awful solemnity, and was forthwith hung.

More or less of this was in some degree necessary. The killing of an Apache was accounted a good day's work, since it probably meant that the murderer of several white men had gone to his doom. To kill a Mexican only meant that another "bad hombre" had gone to his just deserts.

And most of the Mexicans in Arizona in the early days were "bad hombres"—there is no doubt about that. It was they who gave the Mexican such a bad name on the frontier, and it was they who first earned the title "greaser." They were a murderous, treacherous lot of rascals.

In the Wickenburg stage massacre, for instance, it was known that several Mexicans were involved—wood-choppers. One of these Mexicans was hunted for weeks and was caught soon after I arrived in Phoenix. I was running my dance hall when a committee of citizens met in a mass-meeting and decided that the law was too slow in its working and gave the Mexican too great an opportunity to escape. The meeting then resolved itself into a hanging committee, broke open the jail, seized the prisoner from the arms of the sheriff and hung him to the rafters just inside the jail door. That done, they returned to their homes and occupations satisfied that at least one "Greaser" had not evaded the full penalty of his crimes.

Soon after a Mexican arrived in town with a

string of cows to sell. Somebody recognized the cows as ones that had belonged to a rancher named Patterson. The Mexican was arrested by citizens and a horseman sent out to investigate. Patterson was found killed. At once, and with little ceremony, the Mexican with the cattle was "strung up" to the cross of a gatepost, his body being left to sway in the wind until somebody came along with sufficient decency to cut it down.

Talking about lynchings, reminds me of an inci-dent that had almost slipped my mind. Before I went to Wickenberg from Tucson I became partners with a man named Robert Swope in a bar and gambling lay-out in a little place named Adamsville, a few miles below where Florence now is on the Gila River. Swope was tending bar one night when an American shot him dead and got away. The murderer was soon afterward captured in Tucson and lynched in company with two Mexicans who were concerned in the murder of a pawnbroker there.

*   *   *   *

In Phoenix I married my first wife, whose given name was Ruficia. Soon afterwards I moved to Tucson, where, after being awarded one child, I had domestic trouble which ended in the courts. My wife finally returned to Phoenix and, being free again, married a man named Murphy. After this experi-ence I determined to take no further chances with matrimony. However, I needed a helpmate, so I solved the difficulty by marrying Paola Ortega by contract for five years. Contract marriages were universally recognized and indulged in in the West of the early days. My relations with Paola were eminently satisfactory until the expiration of the contract, when she went her way and I mine.

Before I leave the subject of Phoenix it will be well to mention that when I left I sold all my property there, consisting of some twenty-two lots, all in the heart of the city, for practically a song. Six of these lots were situated where now is a big planing mill. Several lots I sold to a German for a span of mules. The German is alive today and lives in Phoenix a wealthy man, simply because he had the foresight and acumen to do what I did not do— hang on to his real estate. If I had kept those twenty-two lots until now, without doing more than simply pay my taxes on them, my fortune today would be comfortably up in the six figures. However, I sold the lots, and there's no use crying over spilled milk. Men are doing today all over the world just what I did then.

I had not been in Tucson long before I built there the largest saloon and dance-hall in the Territory. Excepting for one flyer in Florence, which I shall speak of later on, this was to be my last venture into the liquor business. My hall was modeled after those on the Barbary Coast. It cost "four-bits" and drinks to dance, and the dances lasted only a few minutes. At one time I had thirteen Mexican girls dancing in the hall, and this number was increased on special days until the floor was crowded. I always did good business—so good, in fact, that jealousy aroused in the minds of my rivals finally forced me out. Since then, as I have said, with the single Florence exception, I have not been in the dance-hall business, excepting that I now have at some expense put a ball-room into my hotel at Patagonia, in which are held at times social dances which most of the young folk of the county attend, the liquor element being entirely absent, of course.*

Besides paying a heavy license for the privilege of selling liquor in my Tucson dance hall, I was compelled every morning, in addition, to pay over $5 as a license for the dance-hall and $1.50 collector's fees, which, if not paid out every morning as regularly as clockwork, would have threatened my business. I did not complain of this tax; it was a fair one considering the volume of trade I did. But my patronage grew and grew until there came a day when "Cady's Place," as it was known, was making more money for its owner than any similar establishment in Arizona. The saloon-keepers in Tucson became inordinately jealous and determined to put an end to my "luck," as they called it. Accordingly, nine months after I had opened my place these gentlemen used their influence quietly with the Legislature and "jobbed" me. The license was raised for

*Since this was written the State has abolished the sale of liquor from within its boundaries.

dance halls at one bound to $25 per night. This was a heavier tax than even my business would stand, so I set about at once looking for somebody on whom to unload the property. I claim originality, if not a particular observance of ethics, in doing this.

One day a man came along and, when he saw the crowd in the hall, suggested that I sell him a share in the enterprise.

"No," I replied, "I'll not sell you a share; but, to tell you the truth, I'm getting tired of this business, and want to get out of it for good. I'll sell you the whole shooting-match, if you want to buy. Suppose you stay tonight with my barkeep and see what kind of business I do."

He agreed and I put two hundred dollars in my pocket and started around town. I spent that two hundred dollars to such good purpose that that night the hall was crowded to the doors. The prospective purchaser looked on with blinking eyes at the thought of the profits that must accrue to the owner. Would he buy the place? Would he? Well, say— he was so anxious to buy it that he wanted to pass over the cash when he saw me counting up my takings in the small hours of the morning. The takings were, I remember, $417. But I told him not to be in a hurry, to go home and sleep over the proposition and come back the next day.

After he had gone the collector came around, took his $26.50 and departed. On his heels came my man.

"Do you still want to buy?" I asked him.

"You bet your sweet life I want to buy," he replied.

"You're sure you've investigated the proposition fully?" I asked him.

The customer thought of that four hundred and seventeen dollars taken in over the bar the night before and said he had.

"Hand over the money, then," I said, promptly. "The place is yours."

The next morning he came to me with a lugubrious countenance.

"Well," I greeted him, "how much did you make last night?"

"Took in ninety-six dollars," he answered, sadly. "Cady, why didn't you tell me about that $25 tax?"

"Tell you about it?" I repeated, as if astonished. "Why, didn't I ask you if you had investigated the thing fully? Did I ask you to go into the deal blindfold? It wasn't my business to tell you about any tax."

And with that he had to be content.

* * * *

I was now out of the dance-hall business for good, and I looked about for some other and more prosaic occupation to indulge in. Thanks to the deal I had put through with the confiding stranger with the ready cash, I was pretty well "heeled" so far as money went, and all my debts were paid. Finally I decided that I would go into business again and bought a grocery store on Mesilla street.

The handing out of canned tomatoes and salt soda crackers, however, speedily got on my nerves. I was still a comparatively young man and my restless spirit longed for expression in some new environment. About this time Paola, my contract-wife, who was everything that a wife should be in my opinion, became a little homesick and spoke often of the home she had left at Sauxal, a small gulf-coast port in Lower California. Accordingly, one morning, I took it into my head to take her home on a visit to see her people, and, the thought being always father to the action with me, I traded my grocery store for a buckboard and team and some money, and set forth in this conveyance for Yuma. This was a trip not considered so very dangerous, except for the lack of water, for the Indians along the route were mostly peaceable and partly civilized. Only for a short distance out of Tucson did the Apache hold suzerainty, and this only when sufficient Papagos, whose territory it really was, could not be mustered together in force to drive them off. The Papago Indians hated the Apaches quite as much as the white man did, for the Papago lacked the stamina and fighting qualities of the Apache and in other characteristics was an entirely different type of Indian. I have reason to believe that the Apaches were not originally natives of Arizona, but were an offshoot of one of the more ferocious tribes further

north. This I think because, for one thing, the
facial characteristics of the other Arizona Indians—
the Pimas, Papagos, Yumas, Maricopas, and others
—are very similar to each other but totally different
from those of the various Apache tribes, as was the
language they spoke. The Papagos, Pimas, Yumas,
Maricopas and other peaceable Indian peoples were
of a settled nature and had lived in their respective
territories for ages before the white man came to
the West. The Apache, on the other hand, was a
nomad, with no definite country to call his own and
recognizing no boundary lines of other tribes. It
was owing to Apache depredations on the Papagos
and Pimas that the latter were so willingly enlisted
on the side of the White man in the latter's fight
for civilization.

Reaching Yuma without any event to record that I
remember, we took one of the Colorado River boats
to the mouth of the Colorado, where transfers were
made to the deep-sea ships plying between the Colorado Gulf and San Francisco. One of these steam-
ers, which were creditable to the times, we took to
La Paz. At La Paz Paola was fortunate enough to
meet her padrina, or godfather, who furnished us
with mules and horses with which we reached
Sauxal, Paola's home. There we stayed with her
family for some time.

While staying at Sauxal I went to a fiesta in the
Arroyo San Luis and there began playing cooncan
with an old rancher who was accounted one of the

most wealthy inhabitants of the country. I won from him two thousand oranges, five gallons of wine, seventeen buckskins and two hundred heifers. The heifers I presented to Paola and the buckskins I gave to her brothers to make leggings out of. The wine and oranges I took to La Paz and sold, netting a neat little sum thereby.

Sixty miles from La Paz was El Triunfo, one of the best producing silver mines in Lower California, managed by a man named Blake. Obeying an impulse I one day went out to the mine and secured a job, working at it for some time, and among other things starting a small store which was patronized by the company's workmen. Growing tired of this occupation, I returned to Sauxal, fetched Paola and with her returned to Yuma, or Arizona City, where I started a small chicken ranch a few miles up the river. Coyotes and wolves killed my poultry, however, and sores occasioned by ranch work broke out on my hands, so I sold the chicken ranch and moved to Arizona City, opening a restaurant on the main street. In this cafe I made a specialty of pickled feet—not pig's feet, but bull's feet, for which delicacy I claim the original creation. It was some dish, too! They sold like hot-cakes.

While I was in Lower California I witnessed a sight that is well worth speaking of. It was a Mexican funeral, and the queerest one I ever saw or expect to see, though I have read of Chinese funerals that perhaps approach it in peculiarity. It was while on my way back to Sauxal from La Paz that I met the cortege. The corpse was that of a wealthy rancher's wife, and the coffin was strung on two long poles borne by four men. Accompanying the coffin alongside of those carrying it were about two hundred horsemen. The bearers kept up a jog-trot, never once faltering on the way, each horseman taking his turn on the poles. When it became a man's turn to act as bearer nobody told him, but he slipped off his horse, letting it run wherever it pleased, ran to the coffin, ducked under the pole and started with the others on the jog-trot, while the man whose place he had taken caught his horse. Never once in a carry of 150 miles did that coffin stop, and never once did that jog-trot falter. The cortege followers ate at the various ranches they passed, nobody thinking of refusing them food. The 150 mile journey to San Luis was necessary in order to reach a priest who would bury the dead woman. All the dead were treated in the same manner.

While I was in Yuma the railroad reached Dos Palmas, Southern California, and one day I went there with a wagon and bought a load of apples, which, with one man to accompany me, I hauled all the way to Tucson. That wagon-load of apples was the first fruit to arrive in the Territory and it was hailed with acclaim. I sold the lot for one thousand dollars, making a profit well over fifty per cent. Then with the wagon I returned to Yuma.

On the way, as I was nearing Yuma, I stopped at

Canyon Station, which a man named Ed. Lumley kept. Just as we drove up an old priest came out of Lumley's house crying something aloud. We hastened up and he motioned inside. Within we saw poor Lumley dead, with both his hands slashed off and his body bearing other marks of mutilation. It turned out that two Mexicans to whom Lumley had given shelter had killed him because he refused to tell them where he kept his money. The Mexicans were afterwards caught in California, taken to Maricopa county and there, after trial by the usual method, received the just penalty for their crime.

From Yuma I moved to Florence, Arizona, where I built a dance-hall and saloon, which I sold almost immediately to an Italian named Gendani. Then I moved back to Tucson, my old stamping-ground.

INDIAN WARFARE

When strong men fought and loved and lost,
And might was right throughout the land;
When life was wine and wine was life,
And God looked down on endless strife;
Where murder, lust and hate were rife,
What footprints Time left in the sand!

—WOON.

IN THE seventies and early eighties the hostility of the various Apache Indian tribes was at its height, and there was scarcely a man in the Territory who had not at some time felt the dread of these implacable enemies.

By frequent raids on emigrants' wagons and on freighting outfits, the Indians had succeeded in arming themselves fairly successfully with the rifle of the white man; and they kept themselves in ammunition by raids on lonely ranches and by "jumping" or ambushing prospectors and lone travelers. If a man was outnumbered by Apaches he often shot himself, for he knew that if captured he would probably be tortured by one of the fiendish methods made use of by these Indians. If he had a woman with him it was an act of kindness to shoot her, too, for to her, also, even if the element of torture were absent, captivity with the Indians would invariably be an even sadder fate.

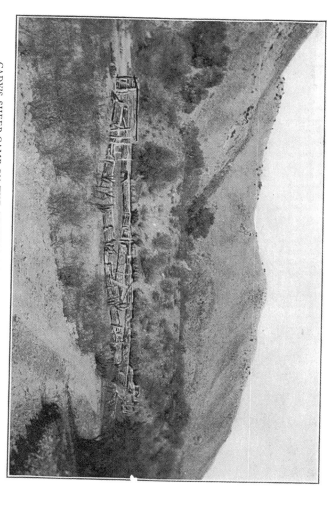

CADY'S SHEEP CAMP ON THE SONOITA, DECEMBER 8, 1914. BUILT IN 1884

Sometimes bands of whites would take the place of the soldiers and revenge themselves on Apache raiders. There was the raid on the Wooster ranch, for instance. This ranch was near Tubac. Wooster lived alone on the ranch with his wife and one hired man. One morning Apaches swooped down on the place, killed Wooster and carried off his wife. As she has never been heard of since it has always been supposed that she was killed. This outrage resulted in the famous "Camp Grant Massacre," the tale of which echoed all over the world, together with indignant protests from centers of culture in the East that the whites of Arizona were "more savage" than the savages themselves. I leave it to the reader to judge whether this was a fact.

The Wooster raid and slaughter was merely the culminating tragedy of a series of murders, robberies and depredations carried on by the Apaches for years. Soldiers would follow the raiders, kill a few of them in retaliation, and a few days later another outrage would be perpetrated. The Apaches were absolutely fearless in the warfare they carried on for possession of what they, rightly or wrongly, considered their invaded territory. The Apache with the greatest number of murders to his name was most highly thought of by his tribe.

When the Wooster raid occurred I was in Tucson. Everybody in Tucson knew Wooster and liked him. There was general mourning and a cry for instant revenge when his murder was heard of. For a long time it had been believed that the Indians wintering on the government reservation at Camp Grant, at the expense of Uncle Sam, were the authors of the numerous raids in the vicinity of Tucson, though until that time it had been hard to convince the authorities that such was the case. This time, however, it became obvious that something had to be done.

The white men of Tucson held a meeting, at which I was present. Sidney R. De Long, first Mayor of Tucson, was also there. After the meeting had been called to order De Long rose and said:

"Boys, this thing has got to be stopped. The military won't believe us when we tell them that their charity to the Indians is our undoing—that the government's wards are a pack of murderers and cattle thieves. What shall we do?"

"Let the military go hang, and the government, too!" growled one man, "Old Bill" Oury, a considerable figure in the life of early Tucson, and an ex-Confederate soldier.

The meeting applauded.

"We can do what the soldiers won't," I said.

"Right!" said Oury, savagely. "Let's give these devils a taste of their own medicine. Maybe after a few dozen of 'em are killed they'll learn some respect for the white man."

Nobody vetoed the suggestion.

The following day six white men—myself, De Long and fierce old Bill Oury among them, rode out of Tucson bound for Tubac. With us we had three Papago Indian trailers. Arrived at the Wooster ranch the Papagos were set to work and followed a trail that led plain as daylight to the Indian camp at Fort Grant. A cry escaped all of us at this justification of our suspicions.

"That settles it!" ground out Oury, between his set teeth. "It's them Injuns or us. And—it won't be us."

We returned to Tucson, rounded up a party consisting of about fifty Papagos, forty-five Mexicans and ourselves, and set out for Camp Grant. We reached the fort at break of day, or just before, and before the startled Apaches could fully awaken to what was happening, or the near-by soldiers gather their wits together, eighty-seven Aravaipa Apaches had been slain as they lay. The Papagos accounted for most of the dead, but we six white men and our Mexican friends did our part. It was bloody work; but it was justice, and on the frontier then the whites made their own justice.

All of us were arrested, as a matter of course, and when word reached General Sherman at Washington from the commander of the military forces at Fort Grant, an order was issued that all of us were to be tried for murder. We suffered no qualms, for we knew that according to frontier standards what we had done was right, and would inevitably have been done some time or another by somebody. We were tried in Judge Titus' Territorial Court, but, to the dismay of the military and General Sherman, who of course knew nothing of the events that had preceded the massacre, not a man in the jury could be found who would hang us. The Territory was searched for citizens impartial enough to adjudge the slaying of a hostile Apache as murder, but none could be found. The trial turned out a farce and we were all acquitted, to receive the greatest demonstration outside the courtroom that men on trial for their lives ever received in Arizona, I think. One thing that made our acquittal more than certain was the fact, brought out at the trial, that the dress of Mrs. Wooster and a pair of moccasins belonging to her husband were found on the bodies of Indians whom we killed. Lieutenant Whitman, who was in command at Fort Grant, and on whom the responsibility for the conduct of the Indians wintering there chiefly rested, was soon after relieved from duty and transferred to another post. General George Crook arrived to take his place late in 1871. The massacre had occurred on the last day of April of that year.

Other raids occurred. Al Peck, an old and valued friend of mine, had several experiences with the Apaches, which culminated in the Peck raid of April 27, 1886, when Apaches jumped his ranch, killed his wife and a man named Charles Owens and carried off Peck's niece. Apparently satisfied with this, they turned Peck loose, after burning the ranch house. The unfortunate man's step-niece was found some six weeks later by Mexican cowpunchers in the Cocoapi Mountains in Old Mexico.

The famous massacre of the Samaniego freight teams and the destruction of his outfit at Cedar Springs, between Fort Thomas and Wilcox, was witnessed by Charles Beck, another friend of mine. Beck had come in with a quantity of fruit and was unloading it when he heard a fusilade of shots around a bend in the road. A moment later a boy came by helter-skelter on a horse.

"Apaches!" gasped the boy, and rode on.

Beck waited to hear no more. He knew that to attack one of Samaniego's outfits there must be at least a hundred Indians in the neighborhood. Un-hitching his horse, he jumped on its back and rode for dear life in the direction of Eureka Springs. Indians sighted him as he swept into the open and followed, firing as they rode. By luck, however, and the fact that his horse was fresher than those of his pursuers, Beck got safely away.

Thirteen men were killed at this Cedar Springs massacre and thousands of dollars' worth of freight was carried off or destroyed. The raid was unex-pected owing to the fact that the Samaniego brothers had contracts with the government and the stuff in their outfit was intended for the very Indians con-cerned in the ambuscade. One of the Samaniegos was slain at this massacre.

Then there was the Tumacacori raid, at Barnett's ranch in the Tumacacori Mountains, when Charlie

Murray and Tom Shaw were killed. Old Man
Frenchy, as he was called, suffered the severe loss
of his freight and teams when the Indians burned
them up across the Cienega. Many other raids
occurred, particulars of which are not to hand, but
those I have related will serve as samples of the
work of the Indians and will show just how it was
the Apaches gained the name they did of being veri-
table fiends in human form.

*   *   *   *

After the expiration of my contract with Paola
Ortega I remained in a state of single blessedness
for some time, and then married Gregoria Sosa, in
the summer of 1879. Gregoria rewarded me with
one child, a boy, who is now living in Nogales. On
December 23, 1889, Gregoria died and in October,
1890, I married my present wife, whose maiden
name was Donna Paz Paderes, and who belongs to
an old line of Spanish aristocracy in Mexico. We
are now living together in the peace and contentment
of old age, well occupied in bringing up and providing for our family of two children, Mary, who
will be twenty years old on February 25, 1915, and
Charlie, who will be sixteen on the same date. Both
our children, by the grace of God, have been spared
us after severe illnesses.

*   *   *   *

To make hundreds of implacable enemies at one
stroke is something any man would very naturally

hesitate to do, but I did just that about a year after I commenced working for D. A. Sanford, one of the biggest ranchers between the railroad and the border. The explanation of this lies in one word—sheep.

If there was one man whom cattlemen hated with a fierce, unreasoning hatred, it was the man who ran sheep over the open range—a proceeding perfectly legal, but one which threatened the grazing of the cattle inasmuch as where sheep had grazed it was impossible for cattle to feed for some weeks, or until the grass had had time to grow again. Sheep crop almost to the ground and feed in great herds, close together, and the range after a herd of sheep has passed over it looks as if somebody had gone over it with a lawnmower.

In 1881 I closed out the old Sanford ranch stock and was informed by my employer that he had foreclosed a mortgage on 13,000 head of sheep owned by Tully, Ochoa and De Long of Tucson. This firm was the biggest at that time in the Territory and the De Long of the company was one of the six men who led the Papagos in the Camp Grant Massacre. He died in Tucson recently and I am now the only white survivor of that occurrence. Tully, Ochoa and De Long were forced out of business by the coming of the railroad in 1880, which cheapened things so much that the large stock held by the company was sold at prices below what it had cost, necessitating bankruptcy.

I was not surprised to hear that Sanford intended to run sheep, though I will admit that the information was scarcely welcome. Sheep, however, at that time were much scarcer than cattle and fetched, consequently, much higher prices. My employer, D. A. Sanford, who now lives in Washington, D. C., was one of the shrewdest business men in the Territory, and was, as well, one of the best-natured of men. His business acumen is testified to by the fact that he is now sufficiently wealthy to count his pile in the seven figures.

Mr. Sanford's wishes being my own in the matter, of course, I did as I was told, closed out the cattle stock and set the sheep grazing on the range. The cattlemen were angry and sent me an ultimatum to the effect that if the sheep were not at once taken off the grass there would be "trouble." I told them that Sanford was my boss, not them; that I would take his orders and nobody else's, and that until he told me to take the sheep off the range they'd stay precisely where they were.

My reply angered the cattlemen more and before long I became subject to many annoyances. Sheep were found dead, stock was driven off, my ranch hands were shot at, and several times I myself narrowly escaped death at the hands of the enraged cattlemen. I determined not to give in until I received orders to that effect from Mr. Sanford, but I will admit that it was with a feeling of distinct relief that I hailed those orders when they came three years later. For one thing, before the sheep business came up, most of the cattlemen who were now my enemies had been my close friends, and it hurt me to lose their esteem. I am glad to say, however, that most of these cattlemen and cowboys, who, when I ran sheep, would cheerfully have been responsible for my funeral, are my very good friends at the present time; and I trust they will always remain so. Most of them are good fellows and I have always admitted that their side had the best argument.

In spite of the opposition of the cattlemen I made the sheep business a paying one for Mr. Sanford, clearing about $17,000 at the end of three years. When that period had elapsed I had brought shearers to Sanford Station to shear the sheep, but was stopped in my intention with the news that Sanford had sold the lot to Pusch and Zellweger of Tucson. I paid off the men I had hired, satisfied them, and thus closed my last deal in the sheep business. One of the men, Jesus Mabot, I hired to go to the Rodeo with me, while the Chinese gardener hired another named Fernando.

Then occurred that curious succession of fatalities among the Chinamen in the neighborhood that puzzled us all for years and ended by its being impossible to obtain a Chinaman to fill the last man's place.

DEPUTY SHERIFF, CATTLEMAN AND FARMER

You kin have yore Turner sunsets,—he never painted one
Like th' Santa Rita Mountains at th' settin' o' th' sun!
You kin have yore Eastern cornfields, with th' crops that never change,
Me—I've all Arizona, and, best o' all, the Range!
                                                    —WOON.

ABOUT this time Sheriff Bob Paul reigned in Tucson and made me one of his deputies. I had numerous adventures in that capacity, but remember only one as being worth recording here.

One of the toughest characters in the West at that time, a man feared throughout the Territory, was Pat Cannon. He had a score of killings to his credit, and, finally, when Paul became sheriff a warrant was issued for his arrest on a charge of murder. After he had the warrant Paul came to me.

"Cady," he said, "you know Pat Cannon, don't you?"

"I worked with him once," I answered.

"Well," returned Paul, "here's a warrant for his arrest on a murder charge. Go get him."

I obtained a carryall and an Italian boy as driver,

in Tucson, and started for Camp Grant. Arrived there I was informed that it was believed Cannon was at Smithy's wood camp, several miles away. We went on to Smithy's wood camp. Sure enough, Pat was there—very much so. He was the first man I spotted as I drove into the camp. Cannon was sitting at the door of his shack, two revolvers belted on him and his rifle standing up by the door at his side, within easy reach. I knew that Pat didn't know that I was a deputy, so I drove right up.

"Hello," I called. "How's the chance for a game of poker?"

"Pretty good," he returned, amiably. "Smithy'll be in in a few moments, John. Stick around—we have a game every night."

"Sure," I responded, and descended. As I did so I drew my six-shooter and whirled around, aiming the weapon at him point blank.

"Hands up, Pat, you son-of-a-gun," I said, and I guess I grinned. "You're my prisoner."

I had told the Italian boy what to do, beforehand, and he now gave me the steel bracelets, which I snapped on Cannon, whose face bore an expression seemingly a mixture of intense astonishment and disgust. Finally, when I had him safely in the carryall, he spat out a huge chew of tobacco and swore.

He said nothing to me for awhile, and then he remarked, in an injured way:

"Wa-al, Johnny, I sure would never have thought it of you!"

He said nothing more, except to ask me to twist him a cigarette or two, and when we reached Tucson I turned him over safely to Sheriff Paul.

*   *   *   *

You who read this in your stuffy city room, or crowded subway seat, imagine, if you can, the following scene:

Above, the perfect, all-embracing blue of the Arizona sky; set flaming in the middle of it the sun, a glorious blazing orb whose beauty one may dare to gaze upon only through smoked glasses; beneath, the Range, which, far from being a desert, is covered with a growth of grass which grows thicker and greener as the rivers' banks are reached.

All around, Arizona—the painted hills, looking as though someone had carefully swept them early in the morning with a broom; the valleys studded with mesquite trees and greasewood and dotted here and there with brown specks which even the uninitiated will know are cattle, and the river, one of Arizona's minor streams, a few yards across and only a couple of feet deep, but swift-rushing, pebble-strew'd and clear as crystal.

Last, but not least, a heterogeneous mob of cowboys and vaqueros, with their horses champing at the bit and eager to be off on their work. In the foreground a rough, unpainted corral, where are more ponies—wicked-looking, intelligent little beggars, but quick turning as though they owned but two legs instead of four, and hence priceless for the work of the roundup. In the distance, some of them quietly and impudently grazing quite close at hand, are the cattle, the object of the day's gathering.

Cowboys from perhaps a dozen or more ranches are gathered here, for this is the commencement of the Rodeo—the roundup of cattle that takes place semi-annually. Even ranches whose cattle are not grazed on this particular range have representatives here, for often there are strays with brands that show them to have traveled many scores of miles. The business of the cowboys* is to round up and corral the cattle and pick out their own brands from the herd. They then see that the unbranded calves belonging to cows of their brand are properly marked with the hot iron and with the ear-slit, check up the number of yearlings for the benefit of their employers, and take charge of such of the cattle it is considered advisable to drive back to the home ranch.

So much sentimental nonsense has been talked of the cruelty of branding and slitting calves that it is worth while here, perhaps, to state positively that the branding irons do not penetrate the skin and serve simply to burn the roots of the hair so that

---

*The term "cowpuncher" is not common in Arizona as in Montana, but the Arizona cowboys are sometimes called "vaqueros."

the bald marks will show to which ranch the calf belongs. There is little pain to the calf attached to the operation, and one rarely if ever even sees a calf licking its brand after it has been applied; and, as is well known, the cow's remedy for an injury, like that of a dog, is always to lick it. As to the ear-slitting, used by most ranches as a check on their brands, it may be said that if the human ear is somewhat callous to pain—as it is—the cow's ear is even more so. One may slice a cow's ear in half in a certain way and she will feel only slight pain, not sufficient to make her give voice. The slitting of a cow's ear draws very little blood.

While I am on the subject,—it was amusing to note the unbounded astonishment of the cattlemen of Arizona a few years ago when some altruistic society of Boston came forward with a brilliant idea that was to abolish the cruelty of branding cows entirely. What was the idea? Oh, they were going to hang a collar around the cow's neck, with a brass tag on it to tell the name of the owner. Or, if that wasn't feasible, they thought that a simple ring and tag put through the cow's ear-lobe would prove eminently satisfactory! The feelings of the cow-boys, when told that they would be required to dismount from their horses, walk up to each cow in turn and politely examine her tag, perhaps with the aid of spectacles, may be better imagined than described. It is sufficient to say that the New England society's idea never got further than Massachusetts, if it was, indeed, used there, which is doubtful.

The brand is absolutely necessary as long as there is an open range, and the abolishment of the open range will mean the abandonment of the cow-ranch. At the time I am speaking of the whole of the Territory of Arizona was one vast open range, over the grassy portions of which cattle belonging to hundreds of different ranches roamed at will. Most of the big ranches employed a few cowboys the year around to keep the fences in repair and to prevent cows from straying too far from the home range. The home range was generally anywhere within a twenty-mile radius of the ranch house.

The ear-slit was first found necessary because of the activities of the rustlers. There were two kinds of these gentry—the kind that owned ranches and passed themselves off as honest ranchers, and the open outlaws, who drove off cattle by first stampeding them in the Indian manner, rushed them across the international line and then sold them to none too scrupulous Mexican ranchers. Of the two it is difficult to say which was the most dangerous or the most reviled by the honest cattlemen. The ranches within twenty or thirty miles of the border, perhaps, suffered more from the stampeders than from the small ranchers, but those on the northern ranges had constantly to cope with the activities of dishonest cattlemen who owned considerably more calves than they had cows, as a rule. The difficulty was to prove that these calves had been stolen.

It was no difficult thing to steal cattle successfully, providing the rustler exercised ordinary caution. The method most in favor among the rustlers was as follows: For some weeks the rustler would ride the range, noting where cows with unbranded calves were grazing. Then, when he had ascertained that no cowboys from neighboring ranches were riding that way, he would drive these cows and their calves into one of the secluded and natural corrals with which the range abounds, rope the calves, brand them with his own brand, hobble and sometimes kill the mother cows to prevent them following their offspring, and drive the latter to his home corral, where in the course of a few weeks they would forget their mothers and be successfully weaned. They would then be turned out to graze on the Range. Sometimes when the rustler did not kill the mother cow the calf proved not to have been successfully weaned, and went back to its mother— the worst possible advertisement of the rustler's dirty work. Generally, therefore, the mother cow was killed, and little trace left of the crime, for the coyotes speedily cleaned flesh, brand and all from the bones of the slain animal. The motto of most of these rustlers was: "A dead cow tells no tales!"

Another method of the rustlers was to adopt a brand much like that of a big ranch near by, and to over-brand the cattle. For instance, a big ranch

CADY AND HIS THIRD FAMILY, 1915

with thousands of cattle owns the brand Cross-Bar (X—). The rustler adopts the brand Cross L (XL) and by the addition of a vertical mark to the bar in the first brand completely changes the brand. It was always a puzzle for the ranchers to find brands that would not be easily changed. Rustlers engaged in this work invariably took grave chances, for a good puncher could tell a changed brand in an instant, and often knew every cow belonging to his ranch by sight, without looking at the brand. When one of these expert cowboys found a suspicious brand he lost no time hunting up proof, and if he found that there had actually been dirty work, the rustler responsible, if wise, would skip the country without leaving note of his destination, for in the days of which I speak the penalty for cow-stealing was almost always death, except when the sheriff happened to be on the spot. Since the sheriff was invariably heart and soul a cattleman himself, he generally took care that he wasn't anywhere in the neighborhood when a cattle thief met his just deserts. Even now this rule holds effect in the cattle lands. Only two years ago a prominent rancher in this country—the Sonoita Range—shot and killed a Mexican who with a partner had been caught red-handed in the act of stealing cattle.

With the gradual disappearance of the open range, cattle stealing has practically stopped, although one still hears at times of cases of the kind, isolated, but bearing traces of the same old methods. Stampeding is, of course, now done away with.

During the years I worked for D. A. Sanford I had more or less trouble all the time with cattle thieves, but succeeded fairly well in either detecting the guilty ones or in getting back the stolen cattle. I meted out swift and sure justice to rustlers, and before long it became rumored around that it was wise to let cattle with the D.S. brand alone. The Sanford brand was changed three times. The D.S. brand I sold to the Vail interests for Sanford, and the Sanford brand was changed to the Dipper, which, afterwards, following the closing out of the Sanford stock, was again altered to the Ninety-Seven (97) brand. Cattle with the 97 brand on them still roam the range about the Sonoita.

*   *   *   *

It was to a rodeo similar to the one which I have attempted to describe that Jesus Mabot and I departed following the incident of the selling of the sheep. We were gone a week. When we returned I put up my horse and was seeing that he had some feed when a shout from Jesus, whom I had sent to find the Chinese gardener to tell him we needed something to eat, came to my ears.

"Oyez, Senor Cady!" Jesus was crying, "El Chino muerte."

I hurried down to the field where Mabot stood and found him gazing at the Chinaman, who was lying face downward near the fence, quite dead. By the smell and the general lay-out, I reckoned he had been dead some three days.

I told Mabot to stay with him and, jumping on my horse, rode to Crittenden, where I obtained a coroner and a jury that would sit on the Chinaman's death. The next morning the jury found that he had been killed by some person or persons unknown, and let it go at that.

Two weeks later I had occasion to go to Tucson, and on tying my horse outside the Italian Brothers' saloon, noticed a man I thought looked familiar sitting on the bench outside. As I came up he pulled his hat over his face so that I could not see it. I went inside, ordered a drink, and looked in the mirror. It gave a perfect reflection of the man outside, and I saw that he was the Mexican Fernando, whom the Chinese gardener had hired when I had engaged Mabot. I had my suspicions right then as to who had killed the Chinaman, but, having nothing by which to prove them, I was forced to let the matter drop.

Two or three years after this I hired as vaquero a Mexican named Neclecto, who after a year quit work and went for a visit to Nogales. Neclecto bought his provisions from the Chinaman who kept the store I had built on the ranch, and so, as we were responsible for the debt, when Bob Bloxton, son-in-law of Sanford, came to pay the Mexican off, he did so in the Chinaman's store.

The next morning Neclecto accompanied Bloxton to the train, and, looking back, Bob saw the Mexican and another man ride off in the direction of the ranch. After it happened Neclecto owned up that he had been in the Chinaman's that night drinking, but insisted that he had left without any trouble with the yellow-skinned storekeeper. But from that day onward the Chinaman was never seen again.

Bloxton persuaded me to return to the ranch from Nogales and we visited the Chinaman's house, where we found the floor dug up as though somebody had been hunting treasure. My wife found a $10 goldpiece hidden in a crack between the 'dobe bricks and later my son, John, unearthed twelve Mexican dollars beneath some manure in the hencoop. Whether this had belonged to the Chinaman, Louey, who had disappeared, or to another Chinaman who had been staying with him, we could not determine. At any rate, we found no trace of Louey or his body.

Even this was not to be the end of the strange series of fatalities to Chinamen on the Sanford ranch. In 1897 I quit the Sanford foremanship after working for my employer seventeen years, and turned the ranch over to Amos Bloxton, another son-in-law of Sanford. I rented agricultural land from Sanford and fell to farming. Near my place Crazy John, a Chinaman, had his gardens, where he made 'dobe bricks besides growing produce.

We were living then in the old store building and

the Chinaman was making bricks about a quarter of a mile away with a Mexican whom he employed. One day we found him dead and the Mexican gone. After that, as was natural, we could never persuade a Chinaman to live anywhere near the place. I later built a house of the bricks the Chinaman was making when he met his death. The Mexican escaped to Sonora, came back when he thought the affair had blown over and went to work for the railroad at Sonoita. There he had a fracas with the section foreman, stabbed him and made off into the hills. Sheriff Wakefield from Tucson came down to get the man and shot him dead near Greaterville, which ended the incident.

In the preceding I have mentioned the railroad. This was the Benson-Hermosillo road, built by the Santa Fe and later sold to the Southern Pacific, which extended the line to San Blas in Coahuila, and which is now in process of extending it further to the city of Tepic. I was one of those who helped survey the original line from Benson to Nogales— I think the date was 1883.

In future times I venture to state that this road will be one of the best-paying properties of the Southern Pacific Company, which has had the courage and foresight to open up the immensely rich empire of Western Mexico. The west coast of Mexico is yet in the baby stage of its development. The revolutions have hindered progress there considerably, but when peace comes at last and those now shouldering arms for this and that faction in the Republic return to the peaceful vocations they owned before the war began, there is no doubt that the world will stand astonished at the riches of this, at present, undeveloped country.   There are portions of the West Coast that have never been surveyed, that are inhabited to this day with peaceful Indians who have seldom seen a white face.   The country is scattered with the ruins of wonderful temples and cathedrals and, doubtless, much of the old Aztec treasure still lies buried for some enterprising fortune-seeker to unearth.   There are also immense forests of cedar and mahogany and other hard woods to be cut; and extensive areas of land suitable for sugar planting and other farming to be brought under cultivation.   When all this is opened up the West Coast cannot help taking its place as a wonderfully rich and productive region.

IN AGE THE CRICKET CHIRPS AND BRINGS—

A faltering step on life's highway,
  A grip on the bottom rung;
A few good deeds done here and there,
  And my life's song is sung.
It's not what you get in pelf that counts,
  It's not your time in the race,
For most of us draw the slower mounts,
  And our deeds can't keep the pace.
It's for each what he's done of kindness,
  And for each what he's done of cheer,
That goes on the Maker's scorebook
  With each succeeding year.

—WOON.

WHILE I was farming on the Sanford ranch a brother-in-law of D. A. Sanford, Frank Lawrence by name, came to live with me. Frank was a splendid fellow and we were fast friends.

One day during the Rodeo we were out where the vaqueros were working and on our return found our home, a 'dobe house, burned down, and all our belongings with it, including considerable provisions. My loss was slight, for in those days I owned a prejudice against acquiring any more worldly goods than I could with comfort pack on my back; but Frank lost a trunk containing several perfectly good suits of clothes and various other more or less valuable articles which he set great store by, besides over a hundred dollars in greenbacks. We hunted among the ruins, of course, but not a vestige of anything savable did we find.

Three days later, however, Sanford himself arrived and took one look at the ruins. Then, without a word, he started poking about with his stick. From underneath where his bed had been he dug up a little box containing several hundred dollars in greenbacks, and from the earth beneath the charred ruins of the chest of drawers he did likewise. Then he stood up and laughed at us. I will admit that he had a perfect right to laugh. He, the one man of the three of us who could best afford to lose anything, was the only man whose money had been saved. Which only goes to prove the proverbial luck of the rich man.

Not long after this experience I moved to Crittenden, where I farmed awhile, running buggy trips to the mines in the neighborhood as a side line.

One day a man named Wheeler, of Wheeler & Perry, a Tucson merchandise establishment, came to Crittenden and I drove him out to Duquesne. On the way Wheeler caught sight of a large fir-pine tree growing on the slope of a hill. He pointed to it and said:

"Say, John, I'd give something to have that tree in my house at Christmas."

It was then a week or so to the twenty-fifth of December.

I glanced at the tree and asked him:

"You would, eh? Now, about how much would you give?"

"I'd give five dollars," he said.

"Done!" I said. "You give me five dollars and count that tree yours for Christmas!" And we shook hands on it.

A few days later I rigged up a wagon, took along three Mexicans with axes, and cut a load of Christmas trees—I think there were some three hundred in the load. Then I drove the wagon to Tucson and after delivering Wheeler his especial tree and receiving the stipulated five dollars for it, commenced peddling the rest on the streets.

And, say! Those Christmas trees sold like wildfire. Everybody wanted one. I sold them for as low as six-bits and as high as five dollars, and before I left pretty nearly everybody in Tucson owned one of my trees.

When I counted up I found that my trip had netted me, over and above expenses, just one thousand dollars.

This, you will have to admit, was some profit for a load of Christmas trees. Sad to relate, however, a year later when I tried to repeat the performance, I found about forty other fellows ahead of me loaded to the guards with Christmas trees of all kinds and sizes. For a time Christmas trees were cheaper than mesquite brush as the overstocked crowd endeavored to unload on an oversupplied town. I escaped with my outfit and my life but no profits—that time.

* * * *

On December 15, 1900, I moved to Patagonia, which had just been born on the wave of the copper boom. I rented a house, which I ran successfully for one year, and then started the building of the first wing of the Patagonia Hotel, which I still own and run, together with a dance-hall, skating rink and restaurant. Since that first wing was built the hotel has changed considerably in appearance, for whenever I got far enough ahead to justify it, I built additions. I think I may say that now the hotel is one of the best structures of its kind in the county. I am considering the advisability of more additions, including a large skating rink and dance-hall, but the copper situation does not justify me in the outlay at present.

I am entirely satisfied with my location, however. Patagonia is not a large place, but it is full of congenial friends and will one day, when the copper industry again finds its feet, be a large town. It is in the very heart of the richest mining zone in the world, if the assayers are to be believed. Some of the mining properties, now nearly all temporarily closed down, are world-famous—I quote for example the Three R., the World's Fair, the Flux, the

Santa Cruz, the Hardshell, the Harshaw, the Hermosa, the Montezuma, the Mansfield and the Mowry.

This last, nine miles from Patagonia, was a producer long before the Civil War. Lead and silver mined at the Mowry were transported to Galveston to be made into bullets for the war—imagine being hit with a silver bullet! In 1857 Sylvester Mowry, owner of the Mowry mine and one of the earliest pioneers of Arizona, was chosen delegate to Congress by petition of the people, but was not admitted to his seat. Mowry was subsequently banished from Arizona by Commander Carleton and his mine confiscated for reasons which were never quite clear.

* * * *

My purpose in writing these memoirs is two-fold: First, I desired that my children should have a record which could be referred to by them after I am gone; and, secondly, that the State of Arizona, my adopted home, should be the richer for the possession of the facts I have at my disposal.

I want the reader to understand that even though the process of evolution has taken a life-time, I cannot cease wondering at the marvelous development of the Territory and, later, State of Arizona. When I glance back over the vista of years and see the old, and then open my eyes to survey the new, it is almost as though a Verne or a Haggard sketch had come to life.

Who, in an uneventful stop-over at Geronimo, Graham county, would believe that these same old Indians who sit so peacefully mouthing their cigarros at the trading store were the terrible Apaches of former days—the same avenging demons who murdered emigrants, fought the modernly-equipped soldier with bow and arrow, robbed and looted right and left and finally were forced to give in to their greatest enemy, Civilization. And who shall begin to conjecture the thoughts that now and again pass through the brains of these old Apache relics, living now so quietly on the bounty of a none-too-generous government? What dreams of settlement massacres, of stage robberies, of desperate fights, they may conjure up until the wheezy arrival of the Arizona Eastern locomotive disperses their visions with the blast of sordid actuality!

For the Arizona that I knew back in the Frontier days was the embodiment of the Old West—the West of sudden fortune and still more sudden death; the West of romance and of gold; of bad whiskey and doubtful women; of the hardy prospector and the old cattleman, who must gaze a little sadly back along the trail as they near the end of it, at thought of the days that may never come again.

And now I myself am reaching the end of my long and eventful journey, and I can say, bringing to mind my youth and all that followed it, that I have *lived,* really *lived,* and I am content.

THE END.